Racism: A Very Short Introduction

Very Short Introductions available now:

For more information visit our web site

www.oup.co.uk/general/vsi/

Ali Rattansi

RACISM

A Very Short Introduction

OXFORD
UNIVERSITY PRESS

OXFORD

UNIVERSITY PRESS

Great Clarendon Street, Oxford OX2 6DP

Oxford University Press is a department of the University of Oxford.
It furthers the University's objective of excellence in research, scholarship,
and education by publishing worldwide in

Oxford New York

Auckland Cape Town Dar es Salaam Hong Kong Karachi
Kuala Lumpur Madrid Melbourne Mexico City Nairobi
New Delhi Shanghai Taipei Toronto

With offices in

Argentina Austria Brazil Chile Czech Republic France Greece
Guatemala Hungary Italy Japan Poland Portugal Singapore
South Korea Switzerland Thailand Turkey Ukraine Vietnam

Oxford is a registered trade mark of Oxford University Press
in the UK and in certain other countries

Published in the United States
by Oxford University Press Inc., New York

© Ali Rattansi 2007

British Library Cataloguing in Publication Data

Data available

Library of Congress Cataloging in Publication Data

Data available

Typeset by RefineCatch Ltd, Bungay, Suffolk
Printed in Great Britain by
Ashford Colour Press Ltd, Gosport, Hampshire

ISBN   978-0-19-280590-4

5 7 9 10 8 6 4

Contents

For Shobhna

Acknowledgements

This book would have been difficult to complete without the generosity of friends and family. Discussions with Avtar Brah, Phil Cohen, Jagdish Gundara, Maxine Molyneux, and Bhikhu Parekh have been a constant source of stimulation and support. My brother Aziz brought his acute intelligence to bear on many of the issues discussed here and gave up much time to enable me to write. Sisters Parin and Zubeida and my mother Nurbanu have been unfailingly encouraging. And Shobhna's love and help have been simply indispensable. I am deeply grateful to them all.

List of illustrations

The publisher and the author apologize for any errors or omissions
in the above list. If contacted they will be pleased to rectify these at
the earliest opportunity.

Introduction

'An important subject about which clear thinking is generally avoided.'

(Ashley Montagu, *Man's Most Dangerous Myth: The Fallacy of Race*, 1954)

A reader expecting easy, cut and dried answers to the questions of what is racism, how it developed, and why it stubbornly continues to survive may be disappointed. But deservedly so. These are large, complex, and contentious issues. Racism is not easy to define, for reasons that will become clear. Short, tight definitions mislead, although in some contexts they are unavoidable. Even in a short book of this kind – perhaps especially in a book that might expect a wide readership – the question of racism requires relatively sophisticated treatment. Brevity and accessibility are not good enough excuses for oversimplification. Although racism is a multidimensional phenomenon, it has suffered from formulaic and clichéd thinking from all sides of the political spectrum. Professional social scientists and historians have been as liable to succumb to the seductions of oversimplification as political activists seeking to mobilize their various constituencies.

My research and writing in this area have been particularly concerned to move discussions of racism away from over-hasty definitions, lazy generalizations, and sloppy analysis. In particular, it is my view that public and academic debates should move away from simplistic attempts to divide racism from non-racism and racists from non-racists. At the risk of exaggeration, I would suggest that one of the main impediments to progress in understanding racism has been the willingness of all involved to propose short, supposedly water-tight definitions of racism and to identify quickly and with more or less complete certainty who is *really* racist and who is not.

Later in the book, I will discuss a number of definitions, including the disastrously confused and unworkable formula popular with many anti-racists: 'Prejudice + Power = Racism'. I will also argue that the idea of institutional racism has outlived its usefulness.

This book, despite being only a very short introduction, is an attempt to present a more nuanced understanding. It also differs from most other introductions to the subject by treating anti-Semitism and anti-Irish sentiments as important elements of any account of racism, and does not assume that racism is simply a property of white cultures and individuals. And it gives due recognition to the fact that racism has always been bound up with a myriad other divisions, especially those of class and gender.

Of course, I have not diluted the many brutal and painful realities that the subject forces us to confront. Millions have died as a result of explicitly racist acts. The injuries and injustices perpetrated in its name continue.

However, most people are nowadays liable to disavow racism. Indeed, the concept of race, as we shall see, has been subject to comprehensive critique within the biological sciences. In the wake of the defeat of Nazism, a great many nation-states have put in place legislative, political, and educative measures to combat racism. Some have introduced programmes such as 'positive action' and 'affirmative action' to undo the effects of past racial discrimination. In its turn, this has provoked a backlash, but which denies any racist intent. On the contrary, the affirmative and positive action programmes have themselves been accused of racism, albeit in reverse.

Confusion abounds. Many accused of racism respond with the argument that their actions and aspirations are to do with patriotism, or that their claims revolve around matters of *ethnic* or *national culture*, not race. To which others add the view that everyone is racist.

However, it is important to bear in mind a distinction between general 'prejudice' and racism properly so-called. That is, no one doubts that humans have always lived in groups and that these collectivities have had some sense of common belonging. The sense of belonging has usually been defined by language, territory, and other markers, which have been used to draw boundaries around the group. They have thus also served to define outsiders and strangers.

But contrary to the common-sense belief that the stranger or outsider inevitably provokes what the French philosopher Pierre-Andre Taguieff calls 'heterophobia', or negative evaluation of the different, the historical and anthropological evidence suggests that outsiders and strangers are not inevitably subjected to hostility. Empathy, curiosity, tolerance, dialogue, and co-operation are human traits that are as common as hostility and prejudice. Outsiders are not automatically feared or hated; they are as likely to be admired, found sexually attractive, to provoke ambivalence, or be envied (as we shall see). And nothing akin to the modern idea of race has been a human universal.

This subject is a minefield indeed. I hope that the reader will emerge a great deal clearer about ways of moving beyond present confusions and unproductive polarizations of position around questions of race and racism.

3

Chapter 1
Racism and racists: some conundrums

The term 'racism' was coined in the 1930s, primarily as a response to the Nazi project of making Germany *judenrein*, or 'clean of Jews'. The Nazis were in no doubt that Jews were a distinct race and posed a threat to the Aryan race to which authentic Germans supposedly belonged.

With hindsight, it is possible to see that many of the dilemmas that have accompanied the proliferation of the notion of racism were present from the beginning. The idea that Jews were a distinct race was given currency by Nazi racial science. But before that, there was little consensus that Jews were a distinct race. Does that make it inappropriate to describe the long-standing hostility to Jews in Christian Europe as racist? Or is it the case that racism has to be seen as a broader phenomenon that has long been part of human history? Indeed, that it is part of 'human nature', and does not necessarily require technical or scientifically sanctioned definitions of 'race' to be identified as racism?

After all, it can be argued that the Nazi project was only one stage in a very long history of anti-Semitism. And that anti-Semitism is one of the oldest racisms, indeed the 'longest hatred', as it has been called.

However, complications immediately arise. The term

'anti-Semitism' only came into being in the late 1870s, when the German Wilhelm Marr used it to characterize his anti-Jewish movement, the Anti-Semitic League, and he used it specifically to differentiate his project from earlier, more diffuse forms of Christian anti-Judaism, more popularly known as *Judenhass*, or 'Jew hatred'. His was a self-conscious racism that required that Jews be defined as a distinct race. And 'Anti-Semitism' had the advantage of sounding like a new, scientific concept separate from simple religious bigotry.

Thus, the key assertion of his little book was that Semitic racial (that is, biological) traits were systematically associated with Jewish character (their culture and behaviour). Jews, according to Marr, could not help but be materialistic and scheming, and these traits meant an inevitable clash with German racial culture, which could not be anything but idealistic and generous. Marr entitled his pamphlet *The Victory of the Jews over the Germans*, because he thought that German racial characteristics meant that Germans would be unable to resist being completely overwhelmed by Jewish cunning. He blamed his own loss of a job on Jewish influence.

Was Marr justified in insisting on distinguishing his version of anti-Jewishness from other historical forms? Is racism properly so-called something totally distinct from the hostility that many would argue is a universal form of suspicion of all 'strangers' and those who have distinct cultural identities? It is after all not uncommon to hear the view that Jews have been particularly prone to victimization because of their own attempts to retain a distinct identity and their refusal to assimilate (one version of the so-called 'Jewish problem'), a type of argument that is often used against other ethnic minorities in European nation-states.

The underlying logic of this sort of viewpoint is that racism is simply part of a continuum that includes, at one end, perfectly understandable and benign collective identifications that are essential for the survival of all cultural groups. At the other end, the

Holocaust and other genocides are therefore to be regarded as unfortunate but inevitable episodes, varying in superficial ways but united by an essential similarity stemming from the very nature of humans as biological and cultural beings who live only in groups, are held together by common feelings of identity, and are thus impelled to maintain their collective identities.

Also, the idea of making the German nation *judenrein* seems close to the notion that has now come to be called 'ethnic cleansing'. But is all 'ethnic cleansing' racist? Or is there something distinctive about racist acts of hatred, expulsion, and violence? In which case, how exactly are we to distinguish between hostility based on ethnicity and that based on race? What is the difference between an ethnic group and a race? To put it somewhat differently, but making the same point, should we distinguish between ethnocentrism and racism?

It is clear that even the briefest inquiry into the meaning of the term 'racism' throws up a number of perplexing questions and various cognate terms – ethnicity and ethnocentrism; nation, nationalism and xenophobia; hostility to 'outsiders' and 'strangers', or heterophobia; and so forth – which require clarification.

There is a further issue that derives from the example of Nazism with which I began. Who exactly is to count as Jewish against whom anti-Semitism could be officially sanctioned? Is there an unambiguous definition? Talmudic law and the immigration policies of the Israeli state accept only those who have Jewish mothers as authentic Jews. This is a strictly biological definition. In Nazi Germany, one had to have three Jewish grandparents to be classified unambiguously as a Jew. Those who were one-fourth and sometimes even half-Jewish could be allowed to be considered to be German citizens provided they did not practise Judaism or marry Jews or other part-Jews. In the absence of clear *biological* evidence, a *cultural* practice, commitment to Judaism, functioned as a *racial* marker.

It has come to light recently that men of partial Jewish descent, *Mischlinge* in Nazi terminology, were allowed with Hitler's explicit permission to serve in the German armed forces during the Second World War. Even more surprisingly, in the postwar period some of these *Mischlinge* went to Israel and served in the Israeli army.

To complicate matters even more, it is worth remembering that historically there has been an ambiguity surrounding Jewish 'whiteness' which still persists to some degree. As we will see, the 'whiteness' of Jews, especially in the USA, as of the Italians and the Irish too, has actually been gradually *achieved* in the 20th century as part of a *social and political process* of inclusion. As 'Semites', Jews were often regarded as not belonging to white races, while it was not uncommon in the 19th century for the English and Americans to regard the Irish as 'black', and for Italians to have an ambiguous status between white and black in the USA.

But who is to count as 'black'? The history of US debates and legislation reveals consistent difficulties in defining the black population. A famous 'one drop' rule was adopted in many Southern states, which implied that any black ancestry, however far back, consigned an individual to the wrong side of the white/black divide, determining (disadvantaging) where s/he could live, what kind of work was available, and whether marriage or even relationships could take place with a white partner. One drop of 'white blood', though, did not carry the same weight in defining racial status.

The idea of racism is obviously closely tied to the concept of race, but it should be clear by now that the more one delves into the history of both notions, the more puzzling they turn out to be.

Several important points emerge from considering the examples of Jews and the Irish, and some of the other groups that are discussed later. Firstly, the idea of 'race' contains both biological and cultural elements, for example skin colour, religion, and behaviour. Secondly, the biological and cultural appear to combine in variable proportions in any definition of a racial group, depending upon the group and the historical period in question. And racial status, as in the 'whitening' of Jews, Irish, and others, is subject to political negotiation and transformation.

Inevitably, therefore, the term 'racism' has also become subject to social forces and political conflict. The idea of race has been in retreat in the second half of the 20th century in the aftermath of the defeat of Nazism and discoveries in the science of genetics. Nowadays, there is a tendency to regard inter-communal hostilities as stemming from issues of *cultural* rather than racial difference.

Many commentators argue that the justification of hostility and discrimination on grounds of culture rather than race is mostly a rhetorical ploy to get round the taboo around racism that has gradually been established in the Western liberal democracies. There is, they contend, a new 'cultural racism' that has increasingly supplanted an older biological racism. 'Islamophobia' has been identified as one of the most recent forms of this new racism. But can a combination of religious and other cultural antipathy be described as 'racist'? Is this not to rob the idea of racism of any analytical specificity and open the floodgates to a conceptual inflation that simply undermines the legitimacy of the idea? These issues are discussed later in the book.

Fewer and fewer people in Western societies will nowadays openly describe themselves as racist. Yet social scientists, politicians, journalists, and members of various communities are apt to claim that these societies are deeply racist. Government agencies continue to collect statistical and other evidence of racial discrimination and use a variety of laws and other instruments to attempt to enforce non-discriminatory codes of conduct.

In Britain, considerable controversy was ignited in 1999 when Lord Macpherson's inquiry into the murder of the black teenager Stephen Lawrence branded the London Metropolitan Police as *institutionally racist*, thus propelling yet another definition into the public domain (although one well known to social scientists and the subject of controversy in an earlier official report, from the Scarman Inquiry into disorders in the London borough of Brixton in 1981).

This has been only one in a whole series of other investigations that has documented systematic and long-standing discrimination against Britain's ethnic minorities in spheres such as housing, and private and public sector employment.

To take just one instance, the British Medical Association published evidence in 2004 that doctors of South Asian origin had been consistently passed over in terms of recruitment, training opportunities, merit awards, and promotion. One medical specialist of Indian origin was paid nearly £1 million in compensation in March 2004 by an industrial tribunal for racial discrimination by the National Health Service. Moreover, another official report in 2004 revealed that black and Asian British citizens do not experience equal treatment with whites as patients of the National Health Service.

Although greeted with disbelief in some quarters, to many this came as no surprise. In 1984, a Commission for Racial Equality investigation had already revealed that London's highly respected St George's Medical School's admission procedures, inscribed into the School's computer software, had systematically penalized British applicants with non-Christian surnames.

Just prior to my starting work on this book, Britain was (again) convulsed by accusations of racism and counter-accusations of 'political correctness' (a regular occurrence in British public life), when Robert Kilroy-Silk, a well known breakfast television presenter and former Labour MP, was suspended by the BBC for publishing derogatory remarks about 'Arabs'. And one Ron Atkinson, a noted football commentator, resigned after he made feruociously anti-black remarks about a footballer during a period when Atkinson thought the microphone was switched off. Interestingly, black and white alike were divided as to whether Atkinson was *really* a racist, given that he had been an important figure in promoting the cause of black footballers. I shall examine both cases in greater detail later in the book.

Similarly, problematic recent cases can be documented in most Western European nation-states and the USA. In Italy, Prime Minister Berlusconi was forced to apologize after describing a German member of the European Parliament as someone who would have made a suitable actor in a film about Nazi concentration camps. Whether the offence caused to the EMP and the German nation could be described as racist was never clarified, but there seemed general agreement that it had racist connotations, especially after Berlusconi's tourism minister subsequently described Germans as 'blonde hyper-nationalists' whose sense of superiority would not survive an intelligence test.

However, in Germany, revulsion against the Nazi past has meant that 'xenophobia' (*Auslanderfeindlichkeit*) rather than racism is the preferred term in German public discourse, raising yet more questions. What is the relationship between 'hostility towards foreigners' and racism?

In the USA, of course, there are continuing examples of controversy over 'race' and racism, in different guises. In 2004, a long-standing member of the Senate, Trent Lotte, had to resign after publicly expressing nostalgia for a previous period of racial segregation. Two criminal trials found the population strongly divided on 'black/white' lines. Prior to his trial and consideration of the evidence by the jury, O. J. Simpson, a well known sportsman, was believed by most whites to be guilty and most blacks not guilty of the murder of his white wife, a verdict in which the jury acquitted him. The acquittal of white police officers seen on camera beating a black motorist, Rodney King, led to widespread 'race' rioting in

Los Angeles in 1992 and the subsequent retrial and conviction of several officers. And controversy continues over the justification for affirmative action policies that can discriminate in favour of black applicants, especially for higher education, to remedy for past unjust discrimination against the black population. How exactly is racism involved in these events and debates in American public life?

It is even more difficult to decide exactly how racism might be involved in, say, the fact that in the USA black men are 10 times more likely to go to prison than whites, and 1 in 20 over the age of 18 is in jail. Or, as revealed in an Amnesty International report of 2004, why black defendants convicted of killing whites have been sentenced to death 15 times more often than white defendants convicted of killing blacks. Also, blacks convicted of killing other blacks in the USA are only half as likely to suffer the death penalty as when they are convicted of killing whites. Is this racism at work? Where does this and similar instances fit into the American, and indeed general, narrative of racism?

Moreover, consider the case of an Englishman, David Tovey, convicted in October 2002 of firearms and explosives offences. His home in rural Oxfordshire was found to contain various types of guns, explosives, and books and videos on how to make bombs, including nailbombs. He had also hidden a sketch map of a mosque, lists of number plates of cars belonging to black and Asian people, sometimes with 'Paki' and 'nigger' scrawled alongside, and correspondence with the far-right British National Party about asylum seekers. He had first come to police attention as the person daubing anti-white graffiti in local areas. Police concluded that the slogans were designed to stir up whites and that he was on the point of conducting a 'one-man race war'.

In denying that he was a racist, Tovey pointed to the fact that he had been married for a number of years to a woman of Chinese descent and had also had a 16-year relationship with a woman of Jamaican origin. The police, though, were in no doubt that Tovey would at some point have used his weapons, presumably against black and Asian people.

Is it the case that the peculiarity of the private life of Tovey is simply an aberration in an otherwise seamless racist identity, or does it contain clues as to complexities in racist identities in general?

Finally, let us return to the notorious anti-Semite Wilhelm Marr, discussed earlier. He had failed to mention in his book that three out of his four wives had been Jewish and that he had a son by one of them. But in the 1890s he broke with the anti-Jewish movements he had done so much to inspire and asked for forgiveness from the Jewish people.

In attempting to interpret these and other puzzles about racism, we must first confront the history of the idea of race. In doing so, we must pay close attention to the ways in which the notion of race, and its associations with skin colour, facial features, and other aspects of physiognomy, has been intertwined, amongst other things, with issues of class, masculinity and femininity, sexuality, religion, mental illness, and the idea of the nation. And, crucially, with the development of science.

Chapter 2

Fear of the dark?: blacks, Jews, and barbarians

By the time Marr penned his diatribe against the Jews in the 1870s, most of the elements of the modern concept of race were already in place. The idea that human biological characteristics such as skin colour, shape of nose, type of hair, and size of skull were associated with ingrained cultural and behavioural traits was well established. It was widely held that level of ability to use reason, capacity for 'civilization' and the arts, and tendencies towards sexual lasciviousness, for example, could all be read off from a study of the outward appearance of human beings.

There was also considerable speculation about the relation between humans, the 'lower races', and apes. Assertions that inferior races were either born of sexual relations between humans and apes, or interbred with apes, or were closer to apes than other humans were commonplace.

But how far back can one trace racial ideas?

The ancient civilizations
Egypt

In Egyptian representational art, non-Egyptians, usually Africans and Asians, are depicted as distinct. Differences are particularly evident in hairstyles and clothes. Some physical differences are also evident. Nubians from further south in Africa are often painted in darker colours. However, there is no evidence that colour was used in an evaluative sense. Nubians were respected for their achievements, especially as skilled archers and military leaders.

The Greeks

It was common practice to distinguish between Greeks and 'barbarians'. 'Barbarian', although a disparaging term, simply denoted someone who did not speak Greek, someone who babbled, could only speak 'barbar'. The key distinction between Greeks and barbarians had nothing to do with physical appearance, still less something as superficial as skin colour. It represented the difference between people who, like the Greeks, accepted an ideal of the political or *politikos*, a combination of citizenship and civic virtue, and those who preferred to live under authoritarian rule.

Perhaps most interesting is Greek *political* and *environmental* determinism, well represented in the writings of Aristotle. Aristotle thought it possible that cold climates produced populations 'full of spirit but deficient in skill and intelligence', and therefore incapable of ruling others, while Asians displayed skill and intelligence but no spirit, and this explained their predisposition to live in subjection and slavery. 'Greek stock' was lucky to occupy an intermediate geographical location, enabling it to combine skill, intelligence, and spirit, and thus the capacity to govern others.

But this also appears to carry the implication that Asiatics and northern Europeans, were they to live for any length of time in favourable conditions, could develop a character that would allow them to practise Greek-style political organization. This is rather different from the biological determinism of modern racial theories.

The Roman Empire

Unlike the Greek empires which it gradually replaced, the Roman Empire (c. 250 BC to 400 AD) came increasingly to be staffed and run by non-Romans from a wide variety of regions and cultural backgrounds. It is also striking that the Emperor Septemus Severus (193–211 AD) was black, as evidenced by a contemporary portrait.

Christianity, anti-Semitism, and the European Middle Ages

It is generally accepted that in the Greek and Roman civilizations, despite some clashes between Jews and non-Jews, especially in Alexandria, there was no systematic persecution of Jews. Jewish communities flourished in North Africa and the Mediterranean.

Christian antipathy to Jews developed only gradually. What some have called 'theological anti-Semitism' first took root in the Byzantine East from the 4th century AD onwards. Notions of Jews as lewd and gluttonous, 'murderers of the Lord' and 'companions of the devil', began to be propounded by Christian preachers.

A more virulent Christian anti-Judaism is apparent from the 8th century. It is around this period that the charge that Jews sought ways to torture and kill individual Christians acquires greater currency. And notions such as the infamous 'Blood Libel' (the belief that Jews used Christian blood, especially from children, for matzos, or unleavened bread, at Passover) also became more widespread.

Two of the greatest disasters to befall European Jews in the medieval period were, firstly, the massacres of 1096 in parts of France and Germany – and subsequently in England – that followed the declaration of the First Crusade in 1095; secondly, their expulsion from Spain in 1492 after the defeat of the Islamic powers by the Christian crusaders.

Although Jews had been practising a variety of occupations, it was the massacres following the Crusades that gradually confined significant proportions of them to usury. In conditions of physical danger and the scarcity of legal tender, Jews found money-lending a convenient means of livelihood. Lending to barons, clergy, and monarchs who craved a luxurious lifestyle made many Jews wealthy.

Medieval and early modern Europe was characterized by frequent, violent popular outbursts against the Jewish communities. The disorders allowed many Christians to rob Jews of their wealth and renege on debts. The disastrous Black Death, the plague that decimated European populations in the 14th century, was often blamed on Jews.

The culmination of the Crusades was the defeat of the Islamic dynasties that had ruled over the Iberian Peninsula for 700 years. Muslim rule had created tolerant, culturally mixed, vibrant cities, the most famous being Cordoba, Seville, and Granada. Jews had thrived in the new climate of cultural dialogue, scholarship, and trade. But on 31 March 1492, the triumphant Catholic monarchs, Ferdinand and Isabella, signed the edict expelling Jews.

Expulsion from Spain led to a new scattering, with Jewish communities dispersing to other Muslim-ruled territories in the Mediterranean. Some migrated to European territories.

However, there is little evidence throughout this long period of any kind of biological determinism. Jewish cultural practices were not seen to be inevitably bound up with Jewish physiology. The fascination with stereotypical Jewish features, that infamous nose, even the Jewish foot, that was common in later centuries seems to have few if any precursors in medieval and early modern Europe.

Nevertheless, Jews who had converted to Christianity to avoid expulsion from Spain, the so-called *conversos*, fell foul of the doctrine of *limpieza de sangre* (purity of blood), which is certainly a proto-racial notion. In the 16th century, certificates of pure blood were often required for membership of a variety of religious and secular associations.

Wildness and blackness in the European imagination

The Middle Ages were characterized by a symbolism that associated otherness with blackness, wildness, and the monstrous. In Christianity, there had developed associations between darkness and evil. Noah's curse that Canaan, his grandson from Ham, would be fated to a life of servitude was one such instance. Ham derives from the Hebrew *Ch'm*, associated with being black and burnt. The story was subsequently used to underpin theories of the origin of Africans and to justify their enslavement.

The medieval popular imagination had also been much exercised by notions of monstrous peoples with bizarre physical features. And anxieties also focused on Wild Men and Wild Women, beings covered in hair and leaves, highly sexed and licentious, and prone to seduce the unwary.

It is important to note how the figure of Wild populations allowed the coalescence of proto-racial themes with those of social class. Wildness, often associated with the lower orders, came to be seen as part of a more general issue of 'breeding', 'stock', and blood. In particular, the aristocracy, threatened by the crumbling of the feudal order, superimposed doctrines of the innate superiority of those with superior breeding and (blue) blood upon other popular anxieties. An early version of the conflation of biology and culture can be seen at work here.

Islam

For the Christian West, Islam's military successes meant its representation as a potent, indeed terrifying, enemy. The image of Islam as a barbaric Other was significant in creating the notion of

Europe as Christian and civilized. But at this stage the opposition to Islam was not racial.

Of course, Islam had its own conceptions of its neighbours. The Arabs were well acquainted with fairer-skinned peoples to the north and relatively darker southern populations. But the various Islamic currents had little by way of specific racial beliefs. Slavery was common in Arab societies where Islam took hold, and while stereotypes of slaves as stupid can be found, these did not appear to have led to any specific identification of particular cultural and territorial populations as naturally inferior and therefore suitable for permanent servitude.

Disparaging conceptions of other peoples and a colour symbolism associating whiteness with goodness and blackness with negative qualities are evident in many Arab and Islamic texts and practices. But no *consistent* conflations of colour, culture, and physiology have been found to exist.

China

Recent scholarship suggests that attitudes to skin colour and bodily characteristics have a long-standing place in Chinese culture. There is evidence that some groups of non-Chinese peoples were regarded as barbarians. Moreover, the Chinese appear to have had some conception of themselves as being yellow or white.

But it is not clear that the colour consciousness of the ancient Chinese can be said to resemble modern racial thinking. The conflation of physical oddity with absence of culture co-existed with the notion that barbarians could acquire civilization with the adoption of appropriate Chinese customs.

South Asia

Modern India, though, is often regarded as one of the most colour-conscious nations on earth. And it has been tempting to ascribe this to the very long-established tradition of caste, which prescribes boundaries of purity and pollution between communities and contains doctrines which restrict occupations to specific groups over generations.

The notion of *varna*, or caste, as used in the oldest Indian text, the *Veda*, does carry implications of colour. And interpretations of ancient India as having been formed by the invasion of lighter-skinned Aryans who subjugated darker Dravidians, also referred to as Dasyus, adds some plausibility to the idea of some form of race consciousness, especially because a term used to describe the Dasyus, *dasa*, later became the word for slave.

However, recent scholarship suggests a more complex picture. Especially, the idea of a single, wholesale invasion by lighter-skinned peoples at some specific period has now been replaced by a view that sees the formation of ancient Indian culture by a very gradual process of mixing with a variety of populations originating from the northern and western regions outside what is now the Indian nation-state.

It is now accepted by serious historians that the distinction between the Aryan *varna* and the *dasa varna* revolved primarily around language, setting the Sanskrit-speaking populations apart from other linguistic groups. The fact that in crucial later texts, such as the *Mahabharata*, key figures are described as having dark complexions also suggests that the race-thinking that was often attributed to early India has little foundation in historical reality.

Chapter 3

Beyond the pale: scientific racism, the nation, and the politics of colour

When Columbus set out on his momentous journey to what he thought was Asia, the significance of the year, 1492, was not lost on him. He wrote at the head of the first journal of his travels:

> In this present year 1492, after your Highnesses have brought to an end the war against the Moors ... in this very month ... your Highnesses ... determined to send me ... to the said regions of India ... Thus after having driven all the Jews out of your realms and dominions, Your Highnesses ... commanded me to set out with a sufficient Armada to ... India.

The year that is often regarded as marking the birth of Western modernity was one symbolized by the expulsion of internal Others and the beginning of the conquest and pillage of those beyond the Christian, 'civilized' world. The significance of the fact that the modern era can be said to begin with acts of proto-racial aggression should not be lost on us. The modernity inaugurated by the voyages has yet to escape fully the shadows cast by the conquests of Spain and the Americas.

The 'Indians' encounter Columbus

The shores on which Columbus landed, as we now know, were far from the 'Indies'. But he was convinced that he had found what he was looking for.

One of the lessons of the history of 'race' is an appreciation of the extent to which European colonizers saw not the cultures of the colonized as they were, but as they expected them to be. Hence the significance of the discussion of European nightmares of monsters and wild tribes, heathens, and those of impure blood.

Columbus was a man of his times. He believed in the one-eyed and men with tails, and mermaids. He claimed to have seen the mermaids on his journeys.

The Caribs and Arawaks who occupied the islands Columbus chanced upon were sophisticated peoples. They were familiar with agriculture, could make pottery of various designs, and were skilled mariners.

Columbus, though, saw a primitive people, unclothed and dark, and therefore close to nature and uncivilized. He recognized they had names for the lands they occupied, but immediately proceeded to give them names of his choosing. They told him they occupied islands. Columbus dismissed this as predictable ignorance, for he had found the continent he had come looking for. He had a passionate double mission: he had come looking for gold and to spread the word of the Christian God.

But contrary to much writing about Europeans' early encounters with the aboriginal populations of the lands they 'discovered', Columbus's reactions were by no means entirely negative. In the absence of knowing their languages, and by reading emotions into their facial expressions according to his conceptions and wishful thinking, Columbus oscillated between seeing the natives as either completely and extraordinarily good or essentially wicked.

For the subsequent history of racism, it is vital to note this constitutive duality and ambivalence, and to understand its characteristically tangential relation to what these strangers might really be like.

The duality was played out in a famous dispute in 16th-century Spain between Bartolome de Las Casas and Juan Gines de Sepulveda, both of whom had been involved in the settlements in the Indies. The dispute attempted to establish which of Columbus's conceptions was correct. The central point at issue concerned the Indians' possession of reason and thus their status as humans. The issue arose because of the significance of the Christian religion in the way all others were perceived. If the natives were fully human, they needed to be converted and treated, if not as equals, at least as belonging to the same species and therefore as capable not only of reason but emotions and pain in the same way as the conquerors.

For Sepulveda, the Indians were non-rational and closer to apes, and could therefore only be useful to the Spanish if they were enslaved. Casas, more sympathetic to the Indians, argued that they possessed reason and could therefore be converted to Christianity. The Spanish could employ them as subjects of the crown.

The dispute was important in deciding the fate of the Indians. The official position of the Catholic Church and the Spanish monarchy was closer to that of Casas. For them, a distinction had to be made between infidels such as the Jews and Muslims, and the Indians, who had never encountered the Gospel and therefore could not be regarded as inherently incapable of Christianity.

The Casas position that 'all the world's races are men' held sway.

Note, however, that Casas did not object to Africans being enslaved and brought to work in the mines and plantations (although he was later to change his mind and condemn the enslavement of blacks). Here we can see also an early version of different attitudes to the Other, one that has persuaded many subsequent students of the subject to insist on the idea that there are a variety of racisms rather than a singular, monolithic combination of discriminatory doctrine and practice.

More importantly, both the Casas and the Sepulveda perspective involved the potential annihilation of the culture of the Indians, for as the French historian Todorov has argued, the Indians were caught in a double-bind built into the logic of this particular either/or. If they were indeed human, their fate was to be converted to Christianity and be provided with an alternative civilization. If they were not fully human, they would be enslaved and their own indigenous culture deemed worthless and expendable.

Race, nature, and gender: the ambiguous legacies of the Enlightenment

It is now generally acknowledged that the term 'race' entered English early in the 16th century. This was also the time when the term was acquiring currency in other European languages, for example '*rassa*' and '*race*' in French, '*razza*' in Italian, '*raca*' in Portuguese, and '*raza*' in Spanish. By the middle of the 16th century, one common meaning was beginning to gain ground. Race began to refer to family, lineage, and breed. In this there was some continuity with the later Middle Ages, for the term had come to signify continuity over generations in aristocratic and royal families.

It was in the 18th-century period of great intellectual fervour and social change, generally referred to as the Enlightenment, that the idea of race began to be incorporated into more systematic meditations on the nature of the world. Europe made a decisive transition to a distinctly modern age, beyond Columbus's Christianity, with the Enlightenment.

The Enlightenment is usually dubbed the Age of Reason. It is regarded as one that enthroned rationality as the highest human capacity. But the emphasis on reason was counter-balanced by an appreciation of pleasure, passion, and the role of emotions, especially in opposition to Christian doctrines.

Subsequent opinion became particularly deeply divided on what was regarded as the scientism of the Enlightenment, with some latter-day critics seeing the period as one that led to the characteristic modern contempt for less technologically advanced cultures and a freeing of science from morality which ultimately nourished the Holocaust.

A key issue here concerns the Enlightenment attitude to 'nature', seen to be one in which the human task was to penetrate its secrets and bend it to human interests. Nature, like the savage, was 'wild' and had to be 'tamed' by the use of technologies derived from the natural sciences.

However, a counter-discourse, particularly concerned with social and political transformation, also proposed that the real task facing modern humans was to learn how to live harmoniously with nature rather than in opposition to it. This was incorporated into what later came to be called the idea of the 'noble savage'.

The period was also characterized, on the part of some of its leading figures, by veneration for the wisdom and civilization of the Orient. China, especially, was admired for its wisdom, technical achievements, and civilization. The great French Enlightenment intellectual Voltaire (1694–1778) went so far as to argue that the civilization of the West 'owes everything' to the East. *Chinoiserie* and *Sinophilia* were notable features of the mid-18th century in France. It became fashionable to have Chinese gardens, porcelain, and even mock Chinese villages.

The 'noble savage'

While most Europeans of the 18th century regarded themselves the most civilized and refined peoples on earth, there were many intellectuals during the same period who found the increasing development of commerce, a rising upper class that had prospered on the backs of this growing trade, and a tendency for conspicuous consumption in the main cities distasteful and superficial. They drew upon depictions of the life of American Indians as a form of paradise before the Fall. *Mundus Novus* (1503) by Amerigo Vespucci, from whom America took its name, was particularly influential.

Amerigo's noble savage, as he came to be called, was characterized by a number of unique freedoms: from clothes, private property, hierarchy or subordination, sexual taboos, and religion. This added up to a perfect 'state of nature'.

The idea of the noble savage, though, remained a minority discourse overwhelmed by descriptions of bestiality and ideas of the closeness of American Indians and Africans to wild apes. It was also overshadowed by the Enlightenment's strong belief in what has come to be called 'The Idea of Progress', the belief that humankind had progressed from a 'rude' and barbaric stage to the contemporary stage of refinement, political liberty, freedom from superstitious forms of religion, and commercial prosperity.

Racial classification and the Enlightenment

The form of rationality that predominated in the Enlightenment was primarily classificatory and the manner in which the idea of race was increasingly pressed into service to make sense of natural variety reflected this classificatory zeal. The central issue that framed the various classificatory schemes was whether all humans were one species.

The most influential of the classificatory systems of the 18th century was produced by the Swedish naturalist Carl Linnaeus. In the volumes of his *Systema Naturae*, published from 1735 onwards, Linnaeus extended his classification of plants and animals to include humans into the animal variety. *Homo sapiens* was united by the ability to mate with all other kinds of humanity, and Linnaeus proposed a four-fold classification of humans: *americanus* (red, choleric, and erect), *europaeus* (white and muscular), *asiaticus* (yellow, melancholic, and inflexible), and *afer* (black, phlegmatic, indulgent). Linnaeus's attempt to find connections between appearance and temperament can also be gauged from the following passages from the 1792 English edition:

> *H. Europaei.* Of fair complexion, sanguine temperament, and brawny form ... Of gentle manners, acute in judgement, of quick invention, and governed by fixed laws ... *H. Afri.* Of black complexion, phlegmatic temperament, and relaxed fibre ... Of crafty, indolent, and careless disposition, and are governed in their actions by caprice.

The classification has clear evaluative judgements built into it. Nevertheless, the concept of race does not have a privileged status in Linnaeus's work and is not used with any consistency. This was true of the period more generally, when ideas of 'race', 'variety', and 'nation' were often used interchangeably.

1. **Troglodyte and Pygmy: examples of Linnaean types**

Blackness, sexuality, and aesthetics

The two greatest philosophers of the 18th century, Immanuel Kant – now regarded by some as the first proper theorist of race – and David Hume, were equally prone to evaluating the moral and intellectual worth of different peoples classified especially by skin colour. Kant proclaimed in 1764: 'This fellow was quite black . . . a clear proof that what he said was stupid.'

Kant drew explicitly on the revised version of David Hume's *On National Characters* (1754), in which the Scottish philosopher confidently announces:

> I am apt to suspect the negroes in general and all species of men (for there are four or five different kinds) to be naturally inferior to the whites. There never was a civilized nation of any other complexion than white . . . No ingenious manufactures amongst them, no arts, no sciences. On the other hand, the most rude and barbarous of the whites, such as the ancient Germans, the present Tartars have still something eminent about them . . . Such a uniform and constant difference could not happen . . . if nature had not made an original distinction between these breeds of men.

Kant and Hume's acquaintance with black people was negligible. But from early in the 16th century, Portuguese, Spanish, and English adventurers had started bringing West Africans to Europe; 1555 is a momentous date in black–white relations in England, nine years before the birth of Shakespeare, and before England had potatoes, tobacco, or tea. That year, one John Lok brought slaves from Guinea.

It soon became fashionable to have black servants at court and in aristocratic households, dressed in the finest clothes to display the wealth of the masters. But by the 1590s, the black presence had become a pawn in domestic politics. During a period of famine and economic recession, Elizabeth I, having herself had a number of black servants, wrote to the lord mayors of the country's main cities 'that there are of late divers blackamores brought into this realm, of which kind of people there are already here to manie . . . those kinds of people should be sente forth of the land'.

Elizabeth's attempted expulsion of blacks was singularly unsuccessful. By the middle of the 18th century, there were perhaps some 20,000 black people living in Scotland and England, including a well-organized community of 10,000 in London, composed of ex-slaves, servants, musicians, and ex-seamen. By the end of the 18th century, several black writers had published books. One of them, Ignatius Sancho, was friendly with a number of prominent literary figures, including Samuel Johnson.

Nevertheless, the dominant image of the black was that of brutishness and bestiality. And the sexual anxieties and repressed desires of the age were projected onto the black male, as in Shakespeare's *Othello*. The myth of the African's large penis was born during this period.

There was, especially, an association between blackness and ugliness, and between beauty and moral virtue. Aesthetics during the 17th and 18th centuries was dominated by the assumption that the ideal form of all human beauty could be found in Greek and Roman art. The most influential historian of art in the 18th century, Johann Joachim Wincklemann, devised a scale of beauty that highlighted certain features of antique sculptures as the embodiment of beauty. Winckelmann regarded the depressed nose as particularly ugly. The African could not but fall foul of this European ideal of beauty and moral worth.

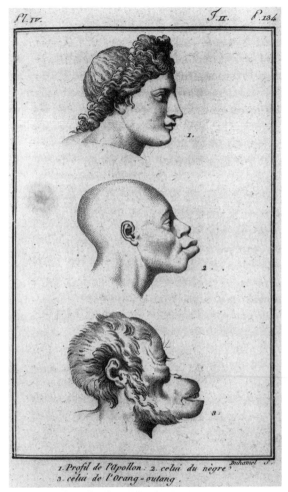

2. A classical Greek profile juxtaposed with those of 'Negro' and ape, purporting to show the similarity between the 'facial angles' of the 'Negro' and those of the ape (1824)

The question of slavery

The question of exactly how much slavery contributed to doctrines of race is a matter of dispute.

British involvement in the slave trade began to take off in the middle of the 17th century, with the formation of the Royal African Company. This trade reinforced the view that the African was sub-human. Thus, African slavery was legitimized by already existing views of Africans as inferior, which were then developed once the institution of African slavery became firmly established.

The growing appetite for sugar, to sweeten the newly popular but bitter beverages of tea, coffee, and chocolate, and the popularity of rum punch fuelled the demand for slave labour on British-owned sugar plantations in the Caribbean. The infamous triangular trade involved ships sailing from Liverpool, Bristol, and London carrying textiles, guns, cutlery, glass, beads, beer, and other British manufactures. These were bartered for slaves on the African coast.

Estimates suggest that at least 20 million able-bodied Africans were crammed into these sailing ships during the whole period of slavery. They were transported across the Atlantic to Jamaica, Barbados, and elsewhere – the notorious 'Middle Passage' – in the most inhumane and oppressive conditions. Large numbers perished in these harsh conditions before they reached their destination and were thrown overboard. The survivors were exchanged for sugar, rum, tobacco, and spices, which were brought back and sold in Britain.

Slavery generated huge amounts of wealth for British traders and planters, and was crucial to the growth of Bristol, Liverpool, and Glasgow. Large fortunes were amassed by slave traders and planters, and played a significant part in ensuring that Britain became the pre-eminent industrial economy, banking centre, and the dominant political and military power in the world.

Slave traders and plantation owners had a crucial interest in representing the black as fit for no other fate. And they claimed a special knowledge of blacks. Edward Long, the son of a Jamaican planter, was typical. He was convinced that 'the lower class of women in England . . . are remarkably fond of the blacks' and worried that 'in the course of a few generations more, the English blood will become so contaminated . . . till the whole nation resembles the Portuguese and Moviscoes in complexion of skin and baseness of mind'. These passages capture the combination of the anxieties posed by class, gender, and race for upper-class males in the 18th century. Long also believed that blacks were a separate species. Unsurprisingly, he drew the conclusion that slavery civilized the African.

The science of race

In the 19th century there emerged a whole range of theories that explained all human variation on the basis of innate racial characteristics. The theories of Robert Knox – who believed that 'race is everything' – published in *The Races of Men* (1850), and the Frenchman Count Arthur de Gobineau, who published his *Essay on the Inequality of Human Races* in 1854, may be taken as typical examples. Such views were united by a variety of assumptions.

Firstly, that humankind could be divided into a limited number of distinct and permanent races, and that race was the key concept for an understanding of human variation. Secondly, that there were distinct physical markers that characterized the different races, especially skin colour, facial features, texture of hair, and, with the growing influence of phrenology, size and shape of skull. Thirdly, that each race was innately associated with distinct social, cultural, and moral traits. Fourthly, that the races could be graded in a coherent hierarchy of talent and beauty, with whites at the top and blacks at the bottom.

A consideration of Gobineau's views highlights other important themes in scientific racism. A reactionary aristocratic critic of the egalitarianism of the French Revolution, Gobineau regarded history as the account of a struggle between different races, white, yellow, and black, but conflates *race with class* so that the history of every 'social order' is the result of conquest by a dominant race, which then forms the nobility, a bourgeois class that is of mixed origins, and a lower class, 'the common people': 'These last belong to a lower race which came about in the south through miscegenation with the negroes and in the north with the Finns.'

The issues of conquest and the racial origins of different classes fed into important streams of hierarchical thinking in the 19th century. There were long-standing beliefs in England, for example, regarding the injustice perpetrated on the Anglo-Saxon people by the Norman invasion. And in France, a popular narrative saw the country as divided between Gauls and the Franks who had invaded in the 5th century

Robert Knox (1791–1862) wanted to convince his contemporaries that the main political conflicts in Europe had an underlying racial basis. He distinguished between Scandinavians, who were supposedly innately democratic, but were incapable of extending democracy to the peoples they subjugated; Celts, who were good fighters but with little political virtue; Slavonians, who had potential but lacked leadership; and the Sarmatians or Russ, who were incapable of real progress in science or literature. True to the principles of the racial theories of the day, though, Knox regarded the darker races as being furthest away from the fair Saxons, and posited that the greatest degree of natural animosity would prevail between these two races.

For the present, two other features of this phase of scientific racism should be noticed. Firstly, many of those involved in trying to prove the inferiority of black and yellow populations were not only against the egalitarian current unleashed with the French Revolution, but were also trying to find scientific justification for the inferiority of women. With the growing popularity of the measurement of skull and brain size, it was often claimed that women's low brain weight and deficient brain structures were similar to those of lower races, and this explained their inferior intellectual abilities.

Moreover, women and the lower races were regarded as being impulsive, emotional, and unable to engage in the abstract reasoning that was the preserve of the white male. This type of analysis allowed a variety of other groups to be denied full civic and political status, for example the sexually deviant and the criminal. Much effort was spent in finding corresponding skull types.

Science and pathology

A related phenomenon was the medicalization of racial analysis, again with strong overtones of sexuality. The two elements combined in the study of black women and prostitutes.

The 19th century's scientific racism sought external signs of the black woman's excessive, animal-like sexuality in the supposedly distinctive appearance of her sexual organs. In 1815, an autopsy was performed on a Saartje Bartmaan, also known as Sarah Bartmann, and more popularly as the 'Hottentot Venus', to reveal more clearly her buttocks and her genitalia. Before her death she had been exhibited to European audiences so that they could gape at her steatopygia, or protruding buttocks. The dissected body was shown so that the lay and medical gaze could also focus on the supposed peculiarities of her genitals.

Medical discourses began to relate studies of the physiology and physiognomy of white prostitutes to analyses of black female bodies to create a powerful chain of association connecting blackness and women's innately pathological sexuality.

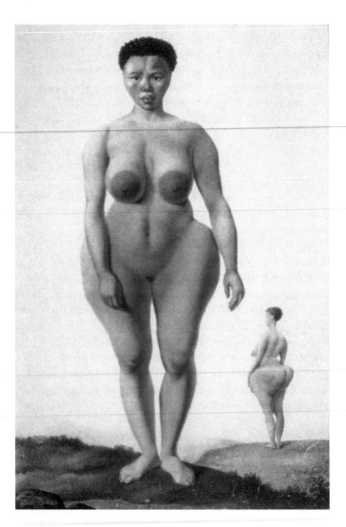

3. A 'Hottentot Venus'

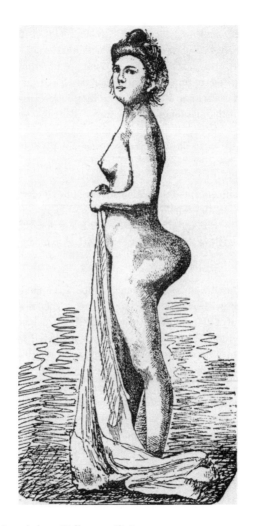

4. **Steatopygia in an Italian prostitute**

Race and nation

The idea of nation has had a crucial role in the origins and development of racial thinking. A contrast between *race* and *nation* was famously made by Johann Gottfried Herder (1744–1803), in a riposte to Kant's essay on the races of mankind. Herder argued that nations were made up of many races. What was important was that over long periods of time each nation had developed a unique culture and civilization, a *Volksgeist*, expressed especially in its language, myths, and songs, a whole way of living that was incommensurate with the cultures of other nations, all of them unique. There was a short distance between notions of *Volkgeist* and racial character.

The 'German' concept of the nation advanced by Herder and the German Romantics, whom he influenced, is often referred to as *Kulturnation*, with its emphasis on *ethnic* bonds. This is distinguished from the *civic* model bequeathed to modernity by the French.

After the 1789 Revolution, the French nation was united by being a voluntary association of free and equal citizens. The French enjoyed membership of the community by virtue of their residence in national territory, irrespective of ethnic origin and religion. But the universalism of the civic models of nationhood was also easily compromised by the particularism of race. In France, national republicans in the 1840s often drew upon the idea of invading Franks oppressing native Gauls. Anti-Semitism too remained a potent force. Fears of a Jewish financial conspiracy against French national interests became an important theme after the collapse of the Union General bank, falsely thought to be owned by Jews. Anti-Semitism became even more highly charged when Captain Alfred Dreyfus, one of the few Jews on the General Staff, was arrested on false spying charges.

Whiteness, blackness, and the promiscuity of 'race'

Above all, the idea of the nation enabled a new boundary between 'them' and 'us' based upon a mixture of people, culture, and race.

This process was facilitated by the fact that no two scientists of race could agree on a classification of races. Skin colours obstinately shaded into each other. Combined with the vagueness of the findings of phrenology and physiognomy, both of which eventually collapsed, a wide range of races were being invented according to the whims of individual racial theorists. Myriad cultural and political traits such as democracy and authoritarianism were arbitrarily attached to races.

Territorial and national concepts, 'Germans' for example, could not be kept strictly separate from racial notions of Teutons and Saxons, or Nordic types. Similar problems were encountered in defining the English, French, or Italian nations.

Elements of social class and sexual difference could also be incorporated. Lower classes and women, just as much as different nations and races, could be denied full membership of the nation because of their supposedly inferior capacity for rationality and self-government when compared to the white, propertied male.

Historically, it did not take long for ideas of nation, race, 'people', citizenship, and popular sovereignty to coalesce. The formation of strong states had a crucial role in this process. As the European nation-states took more definite cultural shape, so the division between the nation's own citizens and foreigners hardened. It was increasingly held that distinctively French, German, and Italian national characteristics had been nurtured by long, shared histories. Thus, non-nationals could be defined as potential invaders or traitors.

The outsider became a potential carrier of pollution who could infect the body politic and damage the nation's health. Conceptions of 'motherland' and 'fatherland' explicitly encouraged associations of biological kinship between citizens of the nation-state. It required no great leap of the imagination to link these themes with miscegenation and racial degeneration through interbreeding between different, incompatible *races*.

The racial theories of Gobineu had diagnosed just such a malaise in post-Revolutionary France. The issues of class and sexuality, always open to incorporation, as we have seen, became intertwined with those of nation and race. Fears about the racial origins and characteristics of the lower classes had been important in post-Enlightenment Europe. Projects of nation-formation had involved the cultural transformation of peasantries and the rapidly growing urban populations of the poor and industrial workers into good French or Italian nationals.

The project of nation-building was also one that involved the gradual imposition of 19th-century 'middle-class' cultures of respectability, family life, hygiene, child-rearing, and sexual behaviour. And conceptions of proper masculinity and femininity, the idea of authentic German or French men and women, were intrinsic to the idea of national character and health.

Not surprisingly, immigrant poor came to be seen as a particular problem. In Britain, the arrival of the Irish, fleeing famine and living in appalling conditions in the cities, provoked virulent racism. There was a widely held view that the Irish were ape-like and innately fond of living in filth, just like their pigs.

Black and white in the USA: the social formation of race and colour

The founding of the USA provides one of the clearest examples of the conflation between race, nation, and citizenship. In 1790, an Act of Congress decreed that 'all free white persons' 'shall be entitled to the rights of citizenship'. While there was some discussion of whether Catholics and Jews should be given the same rights, it seemed so 'natural' to exclude non-whites and women that the subject never came up.

Crucially, the difficulties surrounding racial classification also meant that definitions of black and white remained indeterminate.

The term 'white' had begun as a designation for the European explorers, traders, and settlers who encountered North America's indigenous peoples and, subsequently, Africans. The exclusion of both these groups from membership of the 'civilized', and their dispossession, emerged from the conflation that came to be made between whiteness, work, innate suitability for self-government, and a capacity to defend the republic.

However, it was not long before the seemingly obvious categories of 'white' and 'black' began to throw up their own anomalies. The trigger for what has become a still-surviving anxiety about who is really white in the US was the substantial immigration into the US of *other* kinds of whites to the original settlers. Notions of different white races, already common in Europe, as we have seen, soon proliferated in public discussions in 19th-century America.

The Irish, nearly one and a half million of them, fleeing the terrible famine of the 1840s, soon found themselves at the receiving end of racism from those already settled in the US and who regarded Anglo-Saxon whiteness as superior to that of the Celts.

Some of the descriptions attached to the Irish newcomers are revealing: 'low browed', 'savage', 'bestial', 'lazy', and 'wild' were just some of them. The similarity of this dehumanizing abuse to that directed at blacks and native American populations is obvious. The phrenologist John Beddoe claimed that his systematic study of Irish skulls proved that they were 'Africanoid'. Cartoonists habitually portrayed the Irish as ape-like, images that had been popular in England, accompanying the colonization of Ireland.

TWO FORCES.

5. **Anti-Irish cartoon** (*Punch* 29 October 1881)

6. Equation of blacks and Irish in America. The Irish are depicted as more ape-like (*Harper's Weekly* 9 December 1876)

But the Irish found themselves being increasingly used against black and Chinese workers. Moreover, they began to promote their own whiteness, partly by attacking blacks. They opposed black suffrage and emancipation. They built up formidable political machines, and by the 1890s had come to dominate the white-conscious Democratic Party organizations in the large northern cities.

But the Irish also helped to redefine the idea of the white races to include themselves in a 'Celtic-Anglo-Saxon' race. They promoted a wider unity between people of English, Scotch-Irish, French, Welsh, German, and Irish ancestry as a new and improved American white race.

Subsequently, it was the Italian immigrants – and to some extent the Jews – who found themselves in an indeterminate position in the racial order between white and black. 'Dago' was a common racial slur for describing Italians, accompanied by suggestions of innate emotionality, over-demonstrative behaviour, and 'warped' habits of thought. It was under the umbrella racial category of 'Caucasian' that the Irish, Italians, Polish, Germans, and all other populations of European origin found gradual acceptance as full members of the 'white' American race.

The history of whiteness in the US in the period from the 1840s to the 1940s shows clearly that colour and racial categorization have a fluidity and instability very much at odds with the conceptions of strict and obvious biological difference implied by the notion of race. Moreover, the way in which the category of 'coloured' developed to describe all non-whites serves to highlight the manner in which whiteness became the racial norm in America and elsewhere. The domination by whites in the racial order came to be hidden.

However, blackness, no less than whiteness, has been and continues to be a socially constructed and therefore highly contentious racial description. Eventually, the 'one-drop' rule came to predominate. The idea that any amount of African ancestry meant a classification as black appears to be unique to the US, although in practice similar categorizations have been accepted in the UK and elsewhere.

It has been estimated that at least three-quarters of the black American population has some ancestry that is European or white. Some one-quarter also have American Indian ancestry. Estimates of whites with black ancestry vary widely, from 1% to 20%. All figures are likely to be underestimates, given that much 'mixing' has gone officially undocumented.

It was common for rich white men to have 'mulatto' mistresses in Southern cities during slavery, while on the plantations white slave owners took it for granted that they had legal sexual rights over female slaves.

The status of 'mulattos' – a term derived from the Spanish for 'hybrid' – remained uncertain. A dizzying variety of racial classifications soon emerged in the different states. In Louisiana, 'Creoles' were free, lighter-skinned people of some French or Spanish ancestry. Those who were thought to be seven-eighth African were called 'mango', three-quarters African became 'sambo', and 'meamelou' was applied to anyone with black ancestry.

But criticisms of slavery from the Northern states as well as internationally created a fear of slave insurrection and foreboding about the whole institution of slavery. This led to greater hostility against free blacks of 'mixed' parentage and a tightening of taboos against sexual intercourse between white and black. Vigilante groups – most notoriously the Klu Klux Klan – sprang up in the South in the 1860s to police sexual infractions.

With the end of the Civil War in 1865, in which the continuation of slavery had itself been an issue, the Thirteenth Amendment to the American Constitution was passed, abolishing slavery. In states like

Louisiana, South Carolina, Mississippi, and Arkansas anti-miscegenation laws banning black–white marriages came off the statute books.

But not for long. The continuing hatred of blacks and implacable hostility to their aspirations for equality led to widespread white fears about 'inter-racial' sexual liaisons spiralling out of control, as well as anxieties about economic competition from blacks, who were now officially entitled to learn how to read. Thus, several Southern states adopted the so-called 'Black Codes' which prohibited blacks from entry into industrial and skilled work, confining them to field labour and sharecropping.

It is worth remembering that even in the Northern states before the Civil War blacks were barred from hotels and places of entertainment, from skilled crafts and professional colleges, and segregated on trains and in churches. They had to pay taxes, but could not vote, serve on a jury, or even appear as witnesses in court.

Disastrously, in 1883 a US Supreme Court ruling allowed segregation with regard to all relations involving close personal contact. This allowed Southern states to develop segregated schooling and separate facilities in trains, buses, libraries, parks, swimming pools, and other public amenities. 'Inter-racial' marriages could once again be legally prohibited.

Thus came into being the notorious 'Jim Crow' system of segregation, named after a 'blackface' character, played by whites, portraying blacks as lazy, idiotic, child-like, and happy. The revamped system of segregation was not only legally enforced, but also violently policed by the Klan and other vigilante groups. The lynching of 'uppity' blacks, especially those accused of insulting behaviour towards white women, became horrifyingly common. Between 1890 and 1900, there were over 1,100 lynchings.

Chapter 4
Imperialism, eugenics, and the Holocaust

'Internal' racisms

Ideas of race derived nourishment as much from concerns internal to Europe as from the growing encounters with non-Europeans in the period of early modernity. It should be clear from the discussion in the last chapter that the schemes of classification of human variety that mushroomed in the 18th and 19th centuries were as anxious about drawing boundaries between white European races or 'nations' – Gauls, Saxons, Slavs, and others – as between whites and blacks and Orientals.

Growing nationalisms and a conservative reaction against the collapsing hierarchies of the aristocratic order combined to create fertile breeding grounds for what have sometimes been called 'internal racisms'. Especially, as industrialization began to take off, there were increasing anxieties about the need to control the burgeoning landless labourers flooding into the fast-growing cities. Imperial expansion provided essential intellectual and economic resources in a new social landscape in which class was racialized, and race became intertwined with class and gender in the government of colonial populations. And ideas of race began to exhibit a complexity that cannot be captured in a simple equation between white superiority and non-white inferiority.

Race, class, gender, and empire

The growing industrial working class began to be seen as a 'breed' and 'race' apart from the middle and upper classes. At the same time, the urban slums in which they were forced to live were described in the language of imperialism, as foreign lands full of 'swamps' and 'wilderness', and requiring similar degrees of policing and social control over their degenerate habits.

Moreover, concepts of racial abnormality were superimposed on ideas of sexual and other types of social deviance. Militant sections of the working class, the Irish, Jews, homosexuals, prostitutes, and the insane were regarded as racial deviants. Women who worked, and thus transgressed the Victorian boundary between private and public, were treated as examples of racial regression.

Metaphors of the family, paternalism, and historical progress allowed women, the working class, and inferior races in the colonies alike to be portrayed as child-like and requiring the firm but benign hand of the white middle- and upper-class male. The empire was seen as a 'family', and both women and inferior races thus became part of a natural order ruled over benignly by white middle- and upper-class males at home and abroad.

This went hand in hand with what one might call the effeminization of the natives in the colonies. Colonized lands were given feminine names, Virginia being the most obviously sexualized as well. In large numbers of woodcuts and drawings, the moment of colonization, equated with the beginning of civilization, was symbolized by highly sexually charged images of passive, child-like women encountering upright, handsome white males.

In British imperial projects the effeminization of colonial subjects combined with a class-divided reconstruction of British masculinities. Conceptions of upper-class masculinity, especially of

46

those entrusted with running the empire, institutionalized in the exclusive 'public' schools, emphasized sexual self-restraint and lack of emotional display.

At the same time, the masculinism of imperialism enabled a construction of the middle-class English woman as chaste, frail, and in need of protection, but also precious as the reproducer of an imperial race. This allowed her to be played off against sexually predatory colonial natives and working-class Englishmen as well as the sexually available and erotic 'native' woman, a staple of sexual fantasies fed by narratives published by colonial administrators and the growing number of travellers whose tales of sexual freedoms and exploits, especially in the Orient (including both India and the Arab countries), gained wide circulation.

The sexual attraction of the Oriental woman, especially, introduced a complication in colonial rule that further destabilized the logic of a simple racial inferiorization of dark-skinned races. As William Dalrymple has shown in his *White Moghuls* (2002), in the early stages of British expansion in India, in the 18th century, it was common for British men to adopt Indian modes of dress, to live in dwellings with Indian styles in furnishings, to offer prayers to Indian deities, and to fall in love with and marry Indian women. Homosexuals too found the Orient a more congenial and permissive space.

However, more distant, brutal forms of domination took shape in the 19th century, with the growth of scientific racism and reactions against the resistance offered by hitherto more or less passive natives. The 1857 Indian Mutiny and the 1865 rebellion in Jamaica were particularly influential in inaugurating a more repressive and inferiorizing mode of rule in the colonies.

Even so, the racial logic of colonialism continued to be embedded in an imperial culture in which the Otherness of the colonized was always ambivalent and often contradictory. In the Pacific islands, in a continuation of the noble savage theme, Samoans were seen as attractive, but Fijians were portrayed as savage cannibals.

The British colonial preference for indirect rule through local African and Pacific island chiefs and Indian Nawabs and princes often led to these powerful mediators being seen as equal in some respects. They were given a status commensurate with the aristocratic 'blue-blooded' white governors and administrators. The local notables were often incorporated into colonial culture through the award of titles by the crown, in colourful ceremonies and with resplendent medals and Western military and civilian regalia as worn by the colonial governors, in a form of rule which the British historian David Cannadine has called 'Ornamentalism', to distinguish it from the more pejorative connotations of Edward Said's well known critique of 'Orientalism'.

The case of colonial culture as it developed in India is instructive in exhibiting imperial racism in all its complexity. Conceptions of 'Hindoos' as an inferior race, and Indian society as despotic and stagnant, co-existed with admiration for both Muslim and Hindu architecture and for achievements in the arts and industry, especially the manufacture of textiles. The sexual allure of the Indian woman became an important motif of travel lore. Indian intellectual abilities were highly regarded, leading to the famous proposal by Macaulay in 1835 of an education system for producing 'a class of persons, Indian in blood and colour, but English in taste, opinions, in morals, and in intellect' who would act as 'interpreters between us and the millions whom we govern'.

This led to the setting up of English language schools and universities throughout India, beginning a process of Anglicization that fed into a nationalist movement that was eventually to lead to the overthrow of British rule, while establishing a veneration for English literature in India, especially, which continues to this day.

The study of India's ancient language, Sanskrit, by various scholars, but especially William Jones (1746–94), who founded the Asiatick Society of Bengal, led to the translation of key ancient texts such as the Hindu epic *Bhagavad Gita* and opened up to the European gaze the sophistication of Indian mythology, metaphysics, and religion.

The impact of the Indian texts was even more powerful in Germany, where Romantic intellectuals drew upon Indian sources to nurture their reaction against what they regarded as the excessive rationalism of the (largely French) Enlightenment. The German Idealist movement, of which Herder, Goethe, Schelling, and Schopenhauer were leading lights, was particularly attracted by what its proponents regarded as the parallel philosophical idealism of India, especially the belief that in the final analysis all things form a single whole, that this oneness arises from the fundamentally spiritual nature of reality, the mulitiplicity of things being an illusion produced by limited human senses. Many European scholars believed that all religion and civilization had Indian origins. As Friedrich Schlegel (1772–1829) wrote, 'Everything, yes, everything has its origins in India'.

The veneration was accompanied, however, by doses of primitivism. Indians were also seen as child-like in their innocence and gentle behaviour, and feminine in their supposed deviousness and cowardliness. Sometimes Indian society was interpreted as having decayed from its earlier spirituality into a more greedy and money-obsessed culture, but still retaining sufficient other-worldliness to be unsuitable for the modern world of science and technology.

As becomes clear from Ashis Nandy's brilliant exploration in *Intimate Enemy* (1983), there was no single stereotype, only contradictory ones that characterized European imperial discourses on Indians.

Influenced by the insights of the French social philosopher Michel Foucault (1927–84) into the intertwining of knowledge, power, and rule, especially as deployed in the Arab American cultural critic Edward Said's *Orientalism* (1978) and the new field of 'postcolonialist studies', modern scholars are much more aware of the way colonial knowledges were directly and indirectly implicated in subjugating colonized populations in imperialist projects. Thus, it is now much better understood how the interest shown in Indian culture by the early Orientalists fed directly into notions and practices by which India was governed and Indian culture shaped according to Orientalist preoccupations. Sanskrit was learned as much to allow a better grafting of colonial administration onto indigenous customary laws. In fact, local customs were often only half understood, but were often codified and imposed on locals as their authentic culture.

The nature of the Indian population was documented in myriad surveys and censuses. Most significant in the present context is the British colonial authorities' attempted racial classification of the Indian population.

The division of India into two main races became established as a basis for army recruitment. India was said to be divided between a fair-complexioned, Sanskrit-speaking, martial people of 'Aryan' descent who had made their way from the northwest, and a darker-skinned, inferior race. The 'Aryans' were regarded as a people with European origins, especially because of the notion of a common group of Indo-Aryan and European languages. Aesthetic criteria were also deployed, northern Indian architecture being regarded as closer to Greek classical forms, and indeed as influenced by the Greeks.

Of course, this posed a potential problem about the possible equality of the European colonizers and the Indo-Aryans, an anomaly that was resolved by the suggestion that the original

Aryans had suffered racial degeneration by mixing with the dark-skinned Dravidian and other races. Thus India was linked to Europe's past only in antiquity.

In framing rules for a more direct rule over India after the shock of the 1857 rebellion, British administrators compiled handbooks advising that the more 'martial races' of the Punjab, and subsequently those of Gurkha origin, were the most suitable for recruitment into the army, both on grounds of martial prowess and loyalty to British rule. Only unshorn Sikhs with turbans were regarded as genuine members of the martial races, and this colonial artefact was influential in establishing the turban as a more distinct Sikh emblem in the subsequent identity of Sikhs. 'Effeminate' Bengalis, especially, were kept out.

Racial typologies of Indians became intertwined with caste divisions. The recent historiography of India is now united around the argument that British colonial administrators, in their attempt to classify the Indian population for purposes of more efficient rule, in fact failed to understand the complexity and fluidity of Indian caste divisions. Whereas caste had been one of many social divisions around which the traditional social life of Indians had been organized, together with temple, clan, village, linguistic, and regional identities, overlain with divisions of trade and occupation, the British insisted on a simplified four-caste differentiation and emphasized caste as the most central organizing principle of Indian culture. Only members of the Brahman caste were regarded as being of proper Aryan stock, the other castes being considered as descended from inferior races.

Social Darwinism and imperial racism

The late Victorian era saw a significant cultural realignment. From a period in which gender, race, nation, and class had been closely intertwined emerged a phase in which race assumed a greater importance.

Several factors were responsible. First, there was the coincidence between the Morant Bay black rebellion in Jamaica in 1865 (coming relatively soon after the Indian rebellion of 1857) and the growing momentum of the reform movement for extending the suffrage to much larger sections of the working class. This political mobilization culminated in the 1867 Reform Act, which enfranchised employed, married male householders in Britain.

The result was a more rigid line between whites, deserving of the vote, and the blacks and other natives who – depending on the point of view – were either not ready for enfranchisement or were inherently inferior, could never govern themselves, and were only fit to serve white interests in the British Empire.

Secondly, the idea of empire became part of a widespread popular culture of racism. As trade within the empire grew by leaps and bounds, so advertising, in particular, disseminated even more widely images of blacks as uncivilized, inferior, but smiling, happy, and grateful in their subservience. The empire was charged with 'the white man's burden' of bringing Christianity and civilized habits, especially hygiene, to God's 'coloured' peoples. Particularly striking were the ubiquitous soap advertisements, which equated being 'coloured' with being dirty, a condition which could be metaphorically and literally cleansed away and whitened by the regular use of soap.

Thirdly, the very success of the European, but especially British, imperial project gave widespread legitimacy to the obviousness of white racial superiority, thus including social classes in a joint venture. By 1914, the European powers held 85% of the globe as possessions of one kind or another.

Finally, Social Darwinism and the eugenics movement reinforced the belief in race as the key human division.

7. Gossages' Magical Soap

Eugenics

Charles Darwin held that all humans belonged to the same species. In principle, his *The Origin of Species* (1859), which amongst other things revolutionized understanding on the place of humans in nature, and even more so his *The Descent of Man* (1871), were not reconcilable with the scientific racism of the age. The notion of race rested on the supposition of the characteristics of races remaining stable over time. Darwin's theory of evolution by natural selection privileged change, based on the role of random variations within populations in producing adaptation to changing circumstances.

But his ideas were soon absorbed into prevailing ideas of scientific racism, especially by the group that has come to be called 'Social Darwinists', and subsequently in the policies advocated by the eugenicists. Chief amongst the Social Darwinists was the English sociologist Herbert Spencer (1820–93). It was Spencer who coined the famous phrase 'survival of the fittest', which sanctioned the belief that the technological advances and refined customs of the white races were proof of their greater 'fitness' and the natural necessity that they rule over darker, inferior races.

Social Darwinism nurtured eugenics, a stream of racial thinking that dominated the period from the 1880s to the 1930s in both the US and Europe. A key figure was Francis Galton, cousin of Charles Darwin. A flavour of his views is evident in his belief that English settlers to the US, Canada, and Australia had in effect led to the self-banishment of racially inferior whites, leaving behind 'a better class of Englishmen'.

Galton became especially interested in mapping differing degrees of intelligence amongst human and animal populations. But Galton had no clear means of understanding and assessing intelligence. It is hardly surprising that his 1869 *Hereditary Genius* concluded, on the basis of completely unsystematic observation, that the highest levels of intelligence amongst dogs was greater than that amongst the lowest Australian aborigines, Negroes, Englishmen, and ancient Greeks. Galton and the eugenicists also proposed the doctrine of 'intellectual dysgenesis', which claimed to chart a process of intellectual degeneration in which less intelligent classes reproduced at a higher rate than more intelligent ones. Left unchecked, the result would be an overall dilution of intelligence and a collapse of social institutions. The 'solution' seemed obvious: selective breeding, encouraging classes with higher intelligence to produce more children.

Eugenics attracted support both from prominent liberal and conservative figures of British politics, including the left-leaning Fabians, the Webbs, and Bernard Shaw amongst them.

Two sets of events gave particular impetus to the growth of the movement. Firstly, there was shock in Britain when the poor physical condition of recruits for the Boer War was discovered. Defeat only served to confirm eugenicist fears of racial degeneration. Secondly, in the US, the rapid rise in immigrants who were 'non-Teutonic' or non-'Anglo-Saxon' whites – the Irish, Italians, Poles, Serbs, and Greeks – and then the Chinese, heightened fears that the superior Anglo-Saxons were being swamped by inferior beings with high birth rates.

In 1894, the Immigration Restriction League (IRL) was founded. By 1924, the IRL had succeeded in convincing Congress of the dangers of racial degeneration. The Immigration Act of that year favoured immigration from 'Nordic' countries. The restrictions thus imposed were only finally dismantled by the Cellar Act of 1965, which regulated immigration solely by order of application.

The Nazis and racial genocide: the 'Final Solution'

The Nazi eugenics movement for 'race hygiene' (*Rassenhygiene*) drew many of its intellectual resources from British and American eugenics. But it was not uniformly anti-Semitic. Indeed, between

1904 and 1918 the race hygiene movement contained many Jewish members who supported the programme of improving German genetic stock through selective breeding. There was nothing inevitable about the collapse of German eugenics into the genocidal regime of Hitler and the Nazis.

Recent years have seen an extraordinary resurgence of research on the Holocaust (a term that that only came into widespread use in the late 1950s). We now know more than we have ever done about the minutiae of unfolding events as Hitler's regime hurtled towards the 'Final Solution', the physical extermination of all Jews within their grasp.

Yet this evidence and research are some way from leading to a convincing understanding of how the racist horror of the Holocaust was possible. The events involving the systematic, cold-blooded murder of over six million Jews, 'Gypsies', homosexuals, Slavs, Poles, Communists, and others appears, in the final instance, to be characterized by what some refer to as an incomprehensible 'disruptive excess'.

Was the Holocaust an irrational, barbaric, evil aberration, a collective national psychosis that briefly interrupted the march of a tolerant, liberal, democratic German culture which has otherwise embodied some of the highest ideals of Western civilization?

The Holocaust: some pertinent questions

Posing a number of key questions can allow us to begin a more satisfactory set of inquiries on the German genocide of the Jews and its legacy.

Firstly, to what extent was the attempt to exterminate the Jews primarily the continuation of a long and periodically violent European anti-Semitism that found a hospitable environment in the period between the two World Wars?

Secondly, how central was racist anti-Semitism to Hitler's overall project?

Thirdly, was the 'Final Solution' pre-planned and implemented in a systematic manner by Hitler and his henchmen, and did it flow with an inevitable logic once Nazism acquired power?

Fourthly, a set of related issues need consideration: how many Germans, inside and outside the organized Nazi movement and the armed forces, were actually aware of the systematic murder of the Jews, and what proportion of Germans were actively or tacitly sympathetic to the genocide? To what extent were ordinary Germans racist, and acted as 'willing executioners' for Hitler, as implied in a recent controversial interpretation? How many Germans who voted for Hitler were motivated by racism, and to what extent did they vote for the Nazi Party because of other, more self-interested economic and political concerns?

Finally, what are the implications of the Holocaust for a wider understanding of racism?

Interpreting the Holocaust
Nazism and traditional European anti-Semitism

Nazi anti-Semitism had some features in common with the long tradition of Jew-hatred that had been a marked, though historically intermittent, feature of European culture. As in some previous periods of economic stagnation and decline, it focused on Jews as scapegoats for many of the economic difficulties that emerged after the 1914–18 war, a task made easier by the prominence of some Jews as financiers, retailers, and manufacturers, a relatively rapid growth in Jewish populations, the comparative wealth of even the poorer of these communities, and their high-profile cultural and scientific achievements. Nazi propaganda about Jewish evil also fed on previous anti-Semitic stereotypes of Jews as the murderers of Christ, abductors of

Christians for grisly sacrificial rituals, avaricious money-lenders, and ruthless exploiters of good-natured, hard-working ordinary people. Nazi visual propaganda drew extensively on popular images of Jews as ugly, greedy, venomous parasites, infecting and feeding off the German people, especially peasants. The supposed ugliness of the Jew was constantly contrasted with the regular features of the 'Aryan' race.

8. Typical anti-Semitic image from a 1935 German publication juxtaposing the 'beautiful' Aryan woman and the 'ugly' Jew. The text refers to 'blood libel' and 'racial defilement' as 'original sins'

However, German Jews had enthusiastically embraced German culture and their patriotism was very evident too. Thus the rapid escalation of violent hatred towards them is especially troubling. Even the pre-First World War anti-Semitism of figures such as Marr, Treitschke, and others was flexible enough to allow for the possibility of some Jewish cultural assimilation. The most famous German anti-Semitic precursor of Nazism, the Englishman Houston Stewart Chamberlain, whose *The Foundations of the Twentieth Century* had become a runaway best-seller in 1900, regarded Jewishness as 'a special way of thinking and feeling' which could change as a result of Jews renouncing Judaism.

Not surprisingly, the conclusion of most recent historians is that the Holocaust, despite some of its origins in earlier forms of anti-Semitism, was not an inevitable outcome of it. There was simply not enough lethal venom and deterministic fervour in traditional European anti-Semitism to have led inexorably to a violent attempt at complete extermination.

Western modernity and the Holocaust

Given the firm conclusion that traditional anti-Semitism by itself is a necessary but relatively small part of the explanation for the murderous scale of the Holocaust, most historians and sociologists are now convinced that the Holocaust had several distinctly *modern* characteristics.

Firstly, it was dependent on the emergence of the nation-state. Jews fell foul of specifically modern anxieties about the creation of a nation with enough ethnic homogeneity to sustain a distinct national essence. Secondly, the state acquired a unique social engineering and 'scientific gardening' role in the creation of a 'pure' nation, purged of the human equivalents of weeds and parasites. Thirdly, these gardening analogies were combined with eugenics and other forms of biological determinism to create conceptions of Jews, Gypsies, homosexuals, and others as possessing innate natures that made cultural assimilation impossible. The modern nation-state made Jews, especially, vulnerable to the suspicion that they were an internal quasi-nation, owing their loyalty to global Jewry rather than the nation-state they happened to live in. Thus, traditional forms of anti-Semitism were *racialized*.

Ideas of *racial and political hygiene*, impossible in a pre-modern world view, took strong hold in early 20th-century thinking and policy making, especially in Germany. Their scientists recommended the sterilization, and eventually the extermination, of all groups that supposedly undermined the growth of a pure, strong, healthy, Germanic 'Aryan' race.

Not surprisingly, scientific institutes staffed by distinguished professors of biology, medicine, history, and political science were immediately set up by the Nazis once in power, to resolve 'the Jewish question' in accordance with the latest scientific advances. Talk of dealing with Jews as 'lice' and 'pests', and the process of their removal from the nation as a form of healing (*Gesundung*), became commonplace.

The idea of modern science as a neutral activity enabled many German scientists, some of whom might have known something about what went on in the camps and who might have had misgivings, to sidestep moral qualms involved in the killing of Jews, Gypsies, and homosexuals as part of a project of racial strengthening and purification. The prospect of sophisticated research facilities and the jobs of Jewish scientists who had been killed or forced into exile provided gruesome but attractive incentives to German scientists. Often, research facilities were attached to concentration and death camps, which ensured a steady flow of Jewish and Gypsy twins and the mentally ill for grotesque experiments to be carried out by scientists such as the notorious Dr Mengele.

The amoralism of science dovetailed with the dehumanizing tendencies of modern bureaucracy, which enabled the meticulous

planning and record-keeping of mass murder – amply assisted by
IBM punch-card technology – as a task of no greater significance
than other state projects, with an emphasis on quantification,
efficiency, and a division of labour that meant that functionaries
could follow instructions without feeling the need to question the
wider morality of the tasks they were performing, even if they were
aware, which many were not, that they were taking part in mass
murder. And of course, modern technologies of transportation and
extermination added to the specifically modern character of the
Holocaust.

Hitler's racism

Hitler's rhetoric was replete with images of disease, infection, decay,
and pestilence. He described Jews as decomposing germs and
vermin. 'By exterminating the pest we shall do humanity a service'
was a typical example of Hitler's language. Only modern racial
doctrines could underpin the belief that whole populations carried
an incurable, fatal defect that would perpetuate itself unless
clinically, but ruthlessly, eliminated.

But anti-Semitism only functioned as one element in Hitler's
project of a greater Germany and obtaining revenge for the
humiliating and punitive war reparations imposed on Germany by
the victors of the First World War.

The Holocaust as pre-planned and inevitable

Mass murder, it is now clear, was not the goal of the Nazi movement
from its origins or even by the time, in January 1933, when Hitler
became Chancellor and the Nazi Party gained control over state
apparatuses of violence and possible mass murder.

Certainly, anti-Jewish laws were promulgated from 1933 onwards
that eliminated Jews from the legal and medical professions and
prevented them from inheriting property. The Nuremberg Laws,
within a couple of years, officially titled as being for the
'Protection of German Blood and Honour', attempted precise

legal definitions of Jewry, stripped Jews of their citizenship, and prohibited intermarriage between Jews and 'Aryans'. On 9 November 1938, *Kristallnacht*, a Nazi-inspired night of destruction of Jewish property all over Germany, might be taken as being the prelude to mass murder, but in fact was the beginning of a project of forced mass emigration of Jews and also Poles. The job was entrusted to the newly established Central Office for Jewish Emigration.

At this stage the preferred solution to 'the Jewish question' was *expulsion*, not *extermination*. The Holocaust emerged as a 'Final Solution' at the infamous Wannasee Conference in 1942, only after the Nazis realized that they had no coherent plan for the three million Eastern European Jews who were increasingly being herded into ghettos and living in abysmal conditions.

The German vote for Hitler

Nor should it be assumed that the third of Germans who voted for the Nazis in the 1930s were knowingly voting for genocide. Historians have estimated that perhaps no more than 5% would have voted for Hitler had he stood on a platform of intended war and the Holocaust.

Also, anti-Semitism was only *part* of what the German support for Hitler was based on. In fact, in the big cities where most Jews lived, the Nazis tended to play down their anti-Semitism for fear of alienating voters. Although general hostility to Jews was widespread in Germany, it is arguable that the population at large did not regard Jews, who formed 0.7% of the total population, as the main problem facing the country. The disastrous defeat in the 1914–18 war, the punitive reparations imposed by the victors, and growing unemployment appeared to weigh more heavily in voters' anxieties.

Similarly, latest research reveals that the electoral support that allowed the Nazis to form the largest party in the Reichstag was motivated by a number of factors, anti-Semitism being only one, variable element in a complex and shifting nexus.

Class theories, especially, now have little credibility. There appears to be no overwhelming class bias. Economic sector and religion – first Protestantism and then Catholicism – were the strongest bases for Nazi support. Almost all classes were represented in party membership and electoral support. Working-class support came disproportionately from those in the public sector, reflecting in part the public sector recruitment of military veterans. There is little evidence to suggest that Nazi supporters were more deprived than other workers.

In relation to the middle classes, Nazi support was again strongest in the public services such as higher civil servants, teachers, and other professionals. Small and large business owners were more hospitable to conventional right-wing parties than to the Nazis.

Electoral data and information on Nazi Party membership suggests that a strong motivator for Nazi support was belief in a 'third way', nation-state project that would be above the class interests and battles between large industrialists and the industrial working class. What appealed was the Nazi potential for a form of class-free, strong state modernism. Resentment amongst those who had found themselves expelled from the border areas after the First World War, or generally felt threatened by living in these territories, was also a strong motivation.

The peculiarity of Jewish economic and political positioning, a product of centuries of historical development, also allowed a very particular form of stereotyping and scapegoating.

Jewish success in the worlds of industry and finance was used in mobilizing anti-modernist feelings amongst aristocrats who were already losing out with the increasing collapse of semi-feudal arrangements, whilst allowing a simultaneous appeal to anti-capitalist forces within labour movements.

On the other hand, support from other German upper and middle classes was obtained by highlighting supposedly disproportionate Jewish involvement in left-wing movements in Europe and the Russian Revolution of 1918. The image of the 'Judaeo-Bolshevik' became an important part of Nazi political ideology.

Add the particularity of Jews as a cosmopolitan, worldwide group without a specific homeland, which allowed them to be projected as a race with suspect loyalties to any single nation, and it is not difficult to see why Nazi and anti-Bolshevik fears of a global Jewish conspiracy to dominate the world could gain credibility and allow incorporation into an otherwise biologically based, scientific doctrine of race.

Anti-Semitism, and therefore *racism*, only became effective as a political force in the Nazi rise to power when combined with a whole range of other currents and events, many having very little to do with anti-Semitism *per se*.

Irrationality and paranoia?

But what can be said of the perpetrators? Were those directly and indirectly involved in the killings of Jews deranged, murderous Jew-haters? Were they evil men and women who knew exactly what they were involved with and enjoyed the experience, or at least felt little repugnance in committing mass murder, especially when intoxicated by racism? Was the Holocaust the outcome of an outbreak of madness and irrationalism unlikely to ever happen again?

Although modern bureaucratic procedures may have allowed some functionaries to remain ignorant or keep their distance, there is considerable evidence that key military and bureaucratic officers involved were fully aware of what they were taking part in, once the decision to implement the Final Solution was made.

And there is no evidence that bureaucrats, senior military figures, SS officers, and others involved were insane or suffering from other serious personality disorders. Many of the key figures who were tried at the Nuremberg war crimes tribunals were examined by psychiatrists and pronounced completely sane and 'normal' in every respect. When Eichmann was tried in the 1960s after capture in Argentina, the philosopher Hannah Arendt, who reported on the trial, coined the phrase 'the banality of evil' to capture the sheer ordinariness of the man responsible for so much of the Holocaust.

What seems at first sight remarkable is the manner in which perpetrators involved at various levels of proximity to the killings, including physical acts of violence and torture against Jews, Russians, Poles, Gypsies, homosexuals, and others, were able to compartmentalize their involvement from the rest of their lives. This enabled them to continue to live otherwise normal lives, enjoying their families and friends, having affairs, and celebrating Christmas.

Yet we also know that many of them had serious qualms. Some soldiers and camp officers requested transfers to other duties. Many of those who participated in the killings suffered from what a psychiatrist with the troops called 'psychological decomposition'. Some committed suicide. A large proportion drank to excess.

In part, the project of mass killings survived because of the Nazi movement's success in creating segregated environments where masculine bonding between various levels in the camp hierarchy, alcohol-fuelled camaraderie, opportunities for extras through pitiless robbing of the murdered and the survivors, and the utter degradation and dehumanization of the inmates combined to loosen the physical and moral inhibitions that might otherwise have asserted themselves more forcefully. There was also genuine belief that the gruesome acts were necessary to serve a higher moral purpose, that is, the regeneration of the German nation and race.

Of course, there were many individual acts of kindness towards inmates. We also know from accounts by survivors that affairs between soldiers and Jewish women in the camps were not uncommon.

Hitler's 'willing executioners'?

Something must also be said about the ordinary German citizens, who may or may not have voted for Hitler, but who went through the whole period living normal lives with jobs, families, friends, and whatever possibilities for enjoyment existed while the nation was at war. How much did they know about what was happening to the Jews? What allowed them to keep their heads down and carry on with their lives? Were ordinary Germans 'Hitler's willing executioners' as has been argued in Daniel Goldhagen's best-selling book of 1996?

There is patchy and contradictory evidence about what proportion of the German population was rabidly anti-Semitic, or was fully aware of the killings, or both. However, the bulk of the German population did not object to a lessening of Jewish influence, indeed welcomed it. The laws that removed Jews from the professions and the civil service, and closed down their businesses, seemed to have met with widespread approval.

Some knowledge of the killings was obviously filtering through from soldiers' tales, Allied leaflet drops, and BBC broadcasts. But Hitler's spending on arms and public projects brought jobs and, it seemed, law and order. Most Germans also approved of the reassertion of national power and pride. And there were more pressing worries about food and other shortages, dangers from Allied bombings, and about family and friends fighting at the front lines.

Gestapo informers made dissent hazardous. In concert with the effects of psychological withdrawal and plain indifference, a large number of German citizens were able to carry on their everyday lives without many qualms and without the need to find out more about the fate of Jews and others.

Big businesses like Mercedes Benz profited from the cheap labour of the Jews. It was in their interests to turn a blind eye and most large enterprises reliant on such workers seemed to have little difficulty in ignoring the appalling working conditions while pocketing the profits. Only recently have such companies admitted their culpability and offered compensation to survivors and their families.

The Holocaust: wider implications for racism and racial genocide

The sheer normality of most of those who participated in the mass killings has now led most commentators to argue that when placed in particular circumstances, ordinary human beings are indeed capable of acting with atrocious inhumanity. Varying degrees of racism can combine with a range of other factors to create the conditions for racial and other forms of genocide. Moreover, modern democratic industrial culture not only does not prevent their occurrence, it may actively enable them to be conceived and carried out. The violence can be authorized by legally entitled officials, the murderous activities can be routinized in rule-governed institutions, and the victims can be ideologically dehumanized by modern scientific doctrines.

This interpretation of the Holocaust also raises fundamental issues about the way in which individuals can live with radically different ethical codes, indeed separate 'moral universes' as Katz has put it in his *Confronting Evil* (2004). It seems to be only too possible for people to be loving parents, dedicated scientists, and mass murderers at the same time.

But the Holocaust also demonstrates that the strength of the racism of those who vote for an openly racist party and collaborate or remain passive during such times cannot be simply read off from these actions. It seems likely that large proportions of the German nation were unwitting, or reluctant or unknowing, executioners whose commitment to racism was patchy, weak, and poorly thought through, or non-existent. Racism, even when present, was only one of many motivations that influenced their participation in the nightmare of the Final Solution. And economically deprived populations were not necessarily the most likely to be attracted to racism.

Chapter 5
The case against scientific racism

In the aftermath of the Holocaust and the ending of the Second World War in 1945, the role of eugenics and scientific racism in underpinning the ideology of Nazism was impossible to ignore. Anti-Semitism was only one amongst several forces that eventually led to the murderous project to annihilate Jews. But it was clear that the question of racism and its scientific basis had to be confronted at an international level as part of the attempt to build a successful post-fascist world order.

In July 1950, the newly established UNESCO published a statement that challenged the credibility of scientific racism. The effect of this statement has to be understood in the context of the times. This was a period when, whatever the misgivings about Nazism as a political project, there was widespread popular and academic acceptance of a scientific foundation for the division of humankind into separate races with different, stable, biologically inherited characteristics.

While the UNESCO announcement may have come as a bolt from the blue for large numbers of people, the scientific grounding for this challenge had in fact been in preparation for some time *before* the Holocaust. The interwar period had been characterized by a growing scepticism towards scientific racism. In the US, it came primarily from the newly expanding field of cultural anthropology.

In the UK, the critique emerged largely from biology and other natural sciences.

The early critique of scientific racism

As early as 1911, Franz Boas, based at Columbia University in New York, and who was to become the leading cultural anthropologist of his generation, argued in *The Primitive Mind* that there was no necessary connection between race, language, and culture. Moreover, he argued that there was no fundamental difference between the minds of 'primitives' and the 'civilized'.

His study of the skulls of Italian and Jewish immigrants was especially compelling. Comparing them to those of the populations of origin, he demonstrated that the change in environment led to physical changes in the migrants. The differences between the first and second generations in both populations turned out to be greater than the differences between the original groups of Italians and Jews. Exposure to similar environments in America had narrowed the differences between Italians and Jews. The idea of the stability of the skull, a key thesis of racial science, suffered a fatal blow.

Boas and his students also reanalysed IQ tests conducted by the American army and showed that in fact Northern blacks had outperformed Southern whites. They also undermined the belief in the existence and significance of 'pure' races. Anthropomorphic measurements and detailed genealogies were conducted, which showed that hybrid populations resulting from 'mixture' between blacks and whites displayed a homogeneity which was even greater than that found amongst those of 'pure' European descent.

The pre-eminent position of American eugenics, which generally supported the idea of distinct races and racial hierarchies, also came under attack in the 1930s from British biologists. Huxley and Hogben, social progressives as well as prominent scientists, were key figures in the new critique of eugenics-based race doctrines.

Hogben, the first Professor of Social Biology at the London School of Economics, was instrumental in new statistical studies of IQ tests which suggested that environmental factors could account for as much as 50% of variation in test scores. Also, he pointed out that classification of races based on skin colour or head shape yielded quite different results from typologies using hair texture and nasal index as defining criteria.

Julian Huxley demonstrated that Africans could not be regarded as a single race given the large amount of previous mixing of population groups on the continent and that environmental causes were crucial in explaining the great differences between African cultures.

However, despite the revulsion against Nazi versions of scientific racism, and the new critical voices of the 1930s, it is worth remembering that during the war African American troops had been segregated from white soldiers, their blood supplies were kept separately, and *The Races of Mankind*, a pamphlet in which the anthropologist Ruth Benedict, greatly influenced by Boas, had challenged the idea of white superiority, was banned in the armed forces. Segregation was widely practised in the Southern states in schooling and jobs, and affected the electoral registration of black Americans. In Europe, many Italians were in the grip of ideas about the superiority of the Roman race that had supposedly produced the Roman Empire – and there were plenty of Nazi supporters in Germany. The Japanese, moreover, had made claims to be the 'master race' of Asia.

But throughout the post-1950 period, the work of biologists and social scientists continued to undermine the scientific claims of the category of race.

One key difficulty that exposed the lack of scientificity of the concept was that practically each racial scientist came up with his own bewildering classification of human races. For instance, in

1933 von Eickstedt had come up with a scheme that included three main races, 18 sub-races, three 'collateral' races, as well as three 'intermediate' types. The American defence of racial science by Coon, Garn, and Birdsell had, by the 1950s, yielded the idea of six main stocks and 30 races.

As the early opponents of the concept in the 1930s had pointed out, and as indeed Darwin had done much earlier, whatever the criteria used, the concept of race simply refused to provide unambiguously different types. To put it differently, no 'pure' races could be identified.

Genotype, phenotype, natural selection, and race

It soon became clear where a major problem with racial science was to be found. It had lacked a proper understanding of the implications of the distinction between *genetic* variation in human populations, *phenotypical* differences such as external appearance (skin colour, hair type, shape of nose), and *cultural* and behavioural characteristics as evidenced in belief systems, level of technological development, or political organization. Thus a confused biological determinism had established itself, conflating genes, physiognomy, and culture.

The introduction of the distinction between *genotype* and *phenotype* in 1911 eventually proved seminal. It became accepted that the understanding and assessment of human variation was much more appropriately done at a genotypical rather than phenotypical level. Genotype describes the hereditary potential of an organism. Some genes, for example, are never activated. Others become active in specific environments and at specific times. And genetic make-up can specify how much environmental variation can occur, to produce different phenotypical features. Phenotypical features such as skin colour or shape of nose are now regarded as superficial and irrelevant in judging the real nature and potential of human populations.

In general, a phenotypical variation is a combination of genetic variation and that part of environmental variation that can affect the phenotype. It is crucial to understand the relation between phenotype and processes of natural selection.

Within any particular range of variation, phenotypical features that are best suited to an environment give an organism a selective advantage over others. But biologists can make predictions only in probabilistic terms about the survival chances of types of organism, and always in relation to specific environments. There are no absolute selective advantages regardless of environment.

And the evidence for genetic determination of behaviour is poorly substantiated. Even in dog breeding the connections between genetic similarity and traits such as 'aggressiveness' or 'timidity' are poorly understood.

Gene pool is the appropriate way to understand the distinctiveness of separate groups within a species. Geographical separation over considerable periods of time, and therefore the lack of breeding between populations, is likely to lead to distinctive gene pools, which may be further differentiated if there are relevant variations in environmental conditions.

Cline refers to a measure of the gradient of variations in gene frequency in populations. Differences in clines can reach a point when mating produces infertile offspring. Although human population groups have distinctive clines, no variation has occurred in human populations that prevents one group of humans from breeding with another and successfully continuing the cycle of reproduction. All human populations can interbreed.

Moreover, there are few systematic links between *different types of clinal* variation in human populations. This has profoundly damaging consequences for the idea of race.

For example, blood groups show a relatively systematic variation in an *east–west* distribution. Blood groups A and B are less common in Europe than in Asia. But variation in skin colour follows a *north–south* pattern. Moreover, a person with type A blood could be from Europe, Africa, or Asia. The same is true of a person with type B, O, or AB. All we can conclude is that someone with type B or AB is slightly more likely to have some Asian than African ancestry.

The lack of any systematic connection between genes for blood types and skin colour shows that in humans there is an extraordinarily complex relation between genotype and phenotype. There is no reason to expect consistency of variation in phenotypical characteristics across gene pools, a fact that is obviously lethal for theories of racial classification and hierarchy.

Take the populations of Africa. Although there is a common-sense perception of all Africans as 'black' and as having similar facial features, this is not the case. As anthropologists have pointed out, even in one single area of Africa, for example what is now called the Ivory Coast, there are in fact easily observable differences in skin colour, from light brown to very much darker shades; nose form, from flat to aquiline; and hair colour as well.

In fact, Africa contains the most variation in physical and genetic type on the planet. It has the shortest and tallest people, populations with the thickest and thinnest lips, and very wide differences in width of noses and skull dimensions.

Genetic studies in Africa show a continuous shading of gene frequencies between populations thought to be single 'tribes', as well as genetic similarities between populations thought to be biologically very separate. Indeed, the existence of distinct tribes in Africa has often been traced to arbitrary and convenient administrative and political divisions made by colonial powers.

In genetic science, it is now very widely accepted that genetic variation *within* the groups, that is, amongst the individuals comprising the group, regarded in the past as constituting 'races', is usually greater than the differences *between* the grouped populations. Statistical calculations made by the geneticist Richard Lewontin has revealed that some 85% of genetic variation amongst humans is between individuals in the same population. Another 9% of the variation is between populations that have generally been regarded in previous racial speculations as part of the *same* race. Thus *racial* variation, that is, between populations that have been regarded as belonging to separate races, is only 6%. In any case, this would get slightly smaller or bigger depending upon which racial classification is adopted.

Given the absence of any agreement about the number of so-called races, the only conclusion consistent with genetic analysis is that 'racial' variation is scientifically negligible. There is as yet no evidence to suggest that this 6% makes a substantial difference to the characteristics of different populations. Advocates of race concepts have questioned aspects of Lewontin's analysis, but it is not clear to what degree the idea of race can thereby be rehabilitated.

Given also the failure of phenotypical features such as skin colour, hair type, or shape of nose and skull to provide a systematic and coherent taxonomy of races, the concept of race is now regarded by the majority of biologists as having no credible scientific foundation.

It is not surprising that almost every racial scientist has come up with a unique number and typology of supposed races, nor that anomalies bedevil any attempt to use ordinarily observable characteristics. The continual expansion of the category of 'coloured' in apartheid South Africa to include, eventually, 'Cape Coloured', 'Cape Malay', 'Griqua', 'Indian', 'Chinese', 'other Asiatic', and 'other Coloured' is one of many examples that testify to the absurdities of attempts to provide coherent racial labels.

It is worth noting too that simple evolutionary hypotheses such as the belief that dark skins correlate with exposure to sunlight appear to be, indeed, simplistic. Protection against skin cancer involves far more sophisticated bodily mechanisms than the darker pigmentation produced by melanin. And some of the blackest skins are found in wet, heavily forested populations in West Africa. In the Indian subcontinent, many groups are as dark-skinned as the stereotypical African but have quite different facial features and hair type.

Race and health

Particular diseases have often been associated with distinct population groups. But none of the relevant research findings support the idea of separate *races*. Thalassaemia, often regarded as being most common in those from the Indian subcontinent, is known to occur with great frequency in some Mediterranean regions and South East Asia as well.

Sickle cell anaemia is often thought to be an 'African' or 'black' affliction. But research points to a correlation not with 'race', however defined, but the presence of malaria in an environment. Populations with sickle cell disease appear to have been more likely to survive malaria epidemics, and the genetic predisposition to sickle cell disease was thus passed down the generations. There is little evidence to suggest that the disease originated in West Africa. And it is not solely confined to those who are phenotypically 'black'. Sickle cell disease also occurs among populations with Indian, Arabian, Greek, Turkish, and Italian ancestry.

Osteoporosis is one amongst a host of other significant examples that have been used to shore up the view that humans can be meaningfully divided into distinct races. In bio-medical literature 'Caucasians' and 'Asians' are regarded as having greater propensity to the disease. But this is not a *racial* divide: 'Asian' is a geographical category, while the idea of the 'Caucasian' as a distinct group, as we have seen earlier, has always mixed up biology, geography, and culture.

The confusion here is a product of lack of intellectual rigour, which results in an illegitimate conflation between *biological differentiation on some dimensions* with the vocabulary of *racial* genetics.

What research into diseases confirms is the view that humankind does indeed have populations with distinct commonalities of gene pools, resulting from interbreeding and particular migratory flows. But the pattern of distribution of pools and physiological features simply does not support the idea of separate races.

Race and sport

The modern success of many black athletes and sporting stars has raised once again the spectre of the idea of black bodies being innately more suitable for physical than mental activity. Commonsensical assertions about genetic differences between blacks and whites abound in public discourses about the physical superiority of blacks in sports such as basketball and running events in athletics. The evidence, inevitably, is a lot more complicated.

Although African Americans have excelled at sprint events, Africans have not. In any case, there is no simple correlation between physique and athletic success. While sprinting requires huge muscle power, African Americans more frequently have slim calves.

The success of East African, especially Kenyan, long-distance runners is also intriguing. It has been suggested that the Kenyans have ideal long, slim bodies. But some of the best Kenyan runners have been little more than five foot tall. And we do not have reliable and comprehensive knowledge of what exactly the relationship is between physiological features and running ability, so a fairly large part of the debate rests on mere speculation.

It is also worth noting how research of this type is bedevilled by lack of rigour and absence of genuine comparative data. The findings about Kenyans were derived from a comparison between a number of Swedish and a group of Kenyan long-distance runners. They were compared with regard to enzyme concentrations and other minute biochemical details.

Differences were detected, but it is not clear what conclusions can be drawn from the data. Arguably, living in the highlands has given certain Kenyan populations an advantage. But other populations such as the Tibetans also walk and run at high altitudes without developing the same abilities as the Kenyan highlanders. And any extrapolation of the findings to black–white differences elsewhere, for example in the US, are beset with the problem that very few African Americans are from East Africa and the majority of American whites do not have Scandinavian ancestry. As in other population groups, most of the genetic variation is to be found *within* the Kenyans and Swedes rather than *between* these two groups.

African American domination of basketball appears to have a limited physiological basis, in so far as some studies have suggested that black males jump farther and higher than whites. But whites appear to outperform them in free shooting. This has been attributed to the different sporting *environments* of young whites and blacks in the US rather than to any innate physical differences. White youngsters learn their skills in suburban spaces where they can practise free shooting without competition from other players. Blacks more often play in inner urban areas with overcrowded conditions where they have to work hard at keeping the ball and have to learn to shoot under pressure.

The IQ debate

The earliest versions of tests to measure mental ability were developed in France in 1905 by Alfred Binet, to ascertain the suitability of normal schooling for pupils with learning difficulties. It is the modern IQ debate that has publicly become almost synonymous with the issue of race.

Binet's work was enthusiastically embraced in America and pressed into service by those opposed to the immigration of a variety of ethnic and national groups. Drawing partly on early forms of mental testing, the 1924 Immigration Act restricted the entry of Jews, and Eastern and Southern Europeans.

'Intelligence' was regarded as the appropriate term for mental ability. Research mushroomed, spurred on by the British psychologist Spearman's statistical measures for a *general measure* of a *variety* of mental abilities, as revealed in a range of tests. He labelled this '*g*', which was soon regarded as a summation of an individual's 'intelligence quotient'.

Intelligence has since been regarded as composed of a number of different abilities, for example verbal comprehension, numerical ability, spatial relations, memory, and inductive and deductive reasoning. The notion that a single, measurable quality such as *g* underlies the various components of the tests is based on the assertion that there are significant positive correlations to be found in individual performances on the different tests.

Proponents of IQ testing, such as Herrnstein and Murray, have argued both that high scores correlate with educational achievement and socio-economic success, and that the greater part of intelligence derives from genetic factors rather than environmental context. It is the issue of *heritability* that has proved most controversial, and it is here that the question of race has become most involved.

But it is as well to point out that the relation between IQ scores and socio-economic success is not straightforward either. There is some positive correlation between high IQ, educational achievement, professional advancement, and economic success. But it is not clear that high IQ is a primary *cause* of success and status, as is assumed by the proponents of IQ testing. What causes high individual IQ? Is it an independent variable, on a par with the other factors, or is it itself partly an environmental product of individuals being born into and nurtured by favourable economic and cultural resources within particular family and educational contexts, good schooling, and highly educated parents?

Also, correlations can always be found but may be implausible if interpreted as *causal* relations. For example, positive correlations have been reported between IQ, height, 'altruism', and 'sense of humour'. And the existence of *g* is only one of several different conclusions that can be drawn from the data. Indeed, it has been shown that *g* is a statistical artefact. Many psychometricians have demonstrated that the data is also consistent with the existence of relatively separate abilities or types of intelligence.

Herrnstein, Jensen, and others have asserted that a relatively comprehensive survey of evidence from the US shows on *average* a 15-point difference in IQ performance between blacks and whites. Of course, this also means that many studies have shown a smaller gap while others indicate huge disparities in performance. The wide variation counts against the idea of IQ testing as a precise tool, and indicates the wide range of factors that have to be taken into account when studying the data.

The hereditarians also vary in the weighting they give to genetic determination in explaining differences in IQ scores, from 40% to as much as 80%. This variation is again symptomatic of the weaknesses in the measures and the conceptual underpinning of the genetic argument. This is hardly an exact science.

But there are many other flaws in the hereditarian argument.

For instance, globally, IQ scores have been rising. In Holland and

France, scores have gone up by as much as 25 points between two generations. In the US, the scores of the African American population between 1950 and 1980 rose sufficiently to yield the conclusion that in 1980 their intelligence levels were the same as those of whites in 1950. Given the impossibility of ascribing these changes to rapid genetic transmutations, it is hard to dispute that changes in environmental factors, including better nutrition and education, and other factors deriving from rising standards of living have had a significant impact on performance in the tests.

Nevertheless, the idea that blacks are *inherently* less intelligent than whites and 'Asians' continues to find strong support amongst a vocal minority of psychologists in the US. In the widely cited *Bell Curve*, Herrnstein and Murray argue that the data shows that of the 30 million African Americans, 6 million, or 1 in 5, will have an IQ of 75, which is the threshold for a definition of mental retardation. Only 1 in 20 whites is said to be at this margin. One of their main conclusions is that these are likely to be racial differences and are largely inherited.

But what does a 'black' or African American race actually mean in this context? The black population of America is composed of many different populations, depending upon the mixture of European and Native American, or 'Asian' with African.

Revealingly, Herrnstein and Murray simply discount an important study which found no significant correlation between the amount of genetically detectable white ancestry in black American populations and their IQ scores.

Hereditarians are especially prone to dismiss the impact of generations of racism and social disadvantage on African American educational and professional achievement. The effect of racism is indeed hard to quantify, but the fact that populations of African origin in countries such as Bermuda score as highly as American whites gives clear indication that there is a specificity to the African

American environmental condition that must be taken into account.

Even the black American population that migrated to the North to escape the catastrophic effects of the oppressive racism of the South all too soon found itself trapped in ghettos in de-industrializing areas of Northern cities, cancelling out much of the advantage of leaving the South. Given consistent evidence of the detrimental effects of poor nutrition and degree of intellectual stimulation very early in the lives of children, including a range of experiences in the womb, the case for ascribing a high causal force to the environment in explaining the bulk of the difference between black and white scores is very strong.

The hereditarian position is fatally weakened by the misleading manner in which it deploys the concept of heritability itself. Heritability is a measure of variance in the genetic inheritance of a particular trait, and this too in a specific population, in a given environment at a particular time. Thus, in a population which is uniformly brown eyed entirely because of genetic reasons the heritability is zero (not 100%, which intuition might suggest).

Moreover, because this is an environmentally specific measure, heritability cannot be accurately compared across different populations. So, even if genetic differences were proved to account for 80% of the IQ scores in both black and white *individuals*, this does not allow the inference that *group* differences *between populations* are *genetic* in origin. Herrnstein and Murray admit as much by using as an analogy the consequences of growing seed corn in different environments.

If genetically identical seed corn is planted in two different environments the results could be quite different. As the authors of *The Bell Curve* point out, 'The seeds will grow in Iowa, not in the Mojave [Desert], and the result will have nothing to do with genetic differences.'

Immediately after this statement, Herrnstein and Murray concede that the environment for black Americans has been more like a desert when compared to the social conditions in which whites have lived. This obviously points to a huge environmental rather than genetic effect in determining the different scores of black and white Americans in IQ performance.

But Herrnstein and Murray, illogically, persevere with an interpretation of this analogy in which they draw the conclusion that 60% of the IQ difference between black and white *populations* is genetically determined. Their reasoning is deeply flawed. In effect, they are suggesting that if genetic factors account for 60% of *individual* differences in *white* IQ scores, we can infer that there is a 60% genetic causation of the differences *between black and white group* scores in IQ.

Moreover, Herrnstein and Murray are not consistent in their usage of the concept of race. Elsewhere in *The Bell Curve* their argument leads to the much weaker conclusion that relevant data from around the world shows that it is likely that there are small differences in cognitive ability between 'ethnic' groups. But *ethnicity*, as we shall see, is culturally defined and is not the same as the idea of biologically distinct *races*. There is no warrant for transposing findings from studies of culturally defined groups to 'black' and 'white' or any other *racially* identified population.

Note too that in their discussion of the evidence for 'ethnic' differences in 'cognitive ability', Herrnstein and Murray say that Ashkenazi Jews of European origin are the highest-performing ethnic group. But they ignore evidence that, genetically, Ashkenazi Jews are substantially similar to the Russian and Polish populations amongst whom they have lived.

And in general, as many critics of *The Bell Curve* have pointed out, Herrnstein and Murray underplay or ignore findings from studies which point to significant environmental influences on IQ scores.

It is important to clarify what the critics of the hereditarian position are not claiming. They do not argue that there is *no* genetic element in the determination of various abilities. Thus, nor are they arguing that *all* individual abilities and performances are completely environmentally determined. Their view is that the relationship between genetic inheritance and environmental influence is extremely complicated and that existing data do not allow us to conclude with any precision what differential weighting should be given to genetic or environmental determination. The difficulty, if not impossibility, of devising 'culture-free', or culturally non-biased, tests is also a major stumbling block in making comparisons between different populations.

Crucially, as individual differences cannot enable any conclusions to be drawn about group differences, the edifice of the hereditarian position on race and IQ lacks credible foundation. In turn, the social policies advocated by Herrnstein, Murray, and others, especially the withdrawal of extra funding for the schooling of African American children and the abolition of affirmative action, are also baseless.

And the hereditarian proposition that IQ rather than social factors account for differences in income, rates of crime and unemployment, and births out of wedlock is not warranted by the data. Indeed, Herrnstein and Murray are forced to admit as much in *The Bell Curve*, saying that differences in IQ scores usually account for less than 10%, and sometimes as little as 5%, of the variance in individual achievements, especially socio-economic status. As they put it, 'What this means in English is that you cannot predict what a given person will do from his [sic] IQ score'.

This blatantly contradicts their subsequent argument that 'intelligence itself, not just differences in socioeconomic status' largely account for group differences, while also violating their correct understanding elsewhere in the book that variation in individual IQ scores cannot be transposed to provide data on group differences.

In any case, there is a crucial asymmetry within the concept of ability, which is implicit in Herrnstein and Murray's correct assessment that predictions about individual performance are difficult to make simply from IQ scores. A good performance allows the inference of good ability. But poor performance does not necessarily imply low ability. Ability is one amongst a host of factors that account for bad performance.

Finally, consider the social policy recommendations that some might derive from Herrnstein and Murray's specious reasoning. They warn of the danger that American society will face a growing underclass with a genetically determined low IQ. This population will expand because it is too idiotic to practise birth control. In turn, there will be rising levels of crime and a possibility that city centres will be simply taken over by this underclass. Here, as in so many debates on 'race', the question of class remains strongly intertwined.

The Bell Curve fails to make a credible case for the existence of separate races and the belief that they have genetically differing abilities. The ideas of 'race' and 'racial' hierarchy still have no serious scientific basis.

But if there are no 'races', what meaning can now be given to the concept of 'racism'?

Chapter 6
New racisms?

Few people today, outside the ranks of hard-core members of neo-Nazi and other ultra-right-wing groups, admit to being *racist*.

However, even self-confessed racists appear to have as little agreement about how many races exist and how exactly they are to be differentiated from each other as the supporters of the concept of race in the past. This is simply because humanity cannot be divided into races.

Racism without races?

But if races do not really exist and have never existed, and few people now admit to being racist, what makes it possible for responsible researchers in the social sciences, journalists, politicians, and large numbers of ordinary citizens to claim that racism is still widespread in the contemporary world, especially in Europe and North America?

Indeed, in the last 30 years or so, most Western countries have had to introduce and strengthen laws against forms of racial discrimination. And accusations of racism continue to be regularly made and upheld against individuals, political parties, professional bodies, and other organizations, as evidenced in my first chapter.

Defining race

An unambiguous definition of race would seem to be crucial if claims that racism exists or a racist act has occurred are to be rigorously substantiated. Nowhere is this more vital than in anti-racist legislation, including in the UK, where such anti-discriminatory laws have been defined as 'Race Relations Acts', the first in 1965.

How can race be defined in a context where *racial* discrimination is the target but it is also accepted that 'race' has no scientific foundation?

Let us begin with an important defining case. In 1978, in Britain, under the 1976 Race Relations Act, the parents of a Sikh boy, Gurinder Singh Mandla, brought a prosecution against Park Grove, a private school in Birmingham. The school had refused entry to the boy on the grounds that his turban contravened school uniform rules. In 1983, the House of Lords ruled in favour of the Mandlas.

Especially, in a landmark ruling, it was deemed that Sikhs were a *racial* group because they had a long shared history; cultural traditions of their own; a common geographical origin (or descent from a small number of common ancestors); a common language; a common literature; a common religion; and they were a minority or a majority within a larger community. The House of Lords also argued that a person was a member of a racial group if he or she regarded himself or herself as a member and was accepted as such.

Race and ethnicity

The House of Lords' judgement raises a number of difficult issues that are endemic in attempts to provide credible modern definitions of racism, both in legal and other contexts.

Most crucially, the judgement used primarily *cultural* criteria to define a *racial* group, rather than phenotypical features such as skin colour. It also included the idea of voluntary self-definition, which introduces an extraordinary arbitrariness.

One key difficulty with an exclusively *cultural* definition of a *racial* group is that it makes it impossible to differentiate from the modern idea of *ethnicity*.

But ethnicity too is a problematic concept. *Ethnic* and *ethnicity* derive from the Greek *ethnos*, which refers to a people, a group sharing certain common cultural attributes. In its modern usage, ethnicity assumes the possession of a relatively high degree of coherence and solidarity amongst a group of people who have a conception of common origins, shared culture and experiences, common interests, and participate in some shared activities in which common origin and culture are regarded as significant.

However, as anthropologists, sociologists, and historians have discovered, it is difficult to identify which cultural attributes and shared activities can be taken to define common ethnicity. For example, how important is a common language, and how is this to be weighed as against the possession of a common religion?

And what is to count as a common religion? On some criteria common adherence to Christianity or Islam may be enough. However, in Iraq, Pakistan, and other Muslim countries there is a significant division between Sunni and Shi'a Muslims. In Northern Ireland, despite the commonality of Christianity and the English language, divisions between Protestant and Catholic versions of Christianity have fuelled political and armed conflicts between the two populations.

Ethnicity, like race, is above all a matter of drawing boundaries around zones of *belonging* and *non-belonging*. These include, therefore, *subjective* elements of identity construction, processes of *identification* with particular groups, as well as responses to labels of identity and difference imposed from outside, as in the way Turkey's Muslim identity is emphasized by many in Europe.

Another major problem, however, is encountered by what social scientists call the *situational* and *contextual* nature of ethnic identity construction.

A woman journalist from Wales reporting from India for a British newspaper may accept an Indian's identification of her as 'English', but in Britain may want to emphasize the distinctness of her Welshness. In India or Africa or the Middle East, she may be willing to accept the label 'European', but she may be opposed to membership of the European Union on account of a strong belief in a distinctive British identity and national interests. In other contexts, she may be willing to go along with external labels of her as a 'Westerner', although she may have weak subjective feelings of identification with this broad category.

In Britain today, many people of Pakistani, Muslim origin living in Glasgow identify themselves as 'Scottish Muslims', having absorbed Scottish feelings of animosity towards the English. Others call themselves just Muslims, and have a strong sense of belonging to a global Muslim community, or *Umma*, as their primary point of identification. Some Muslims, though, feel that they are British Muslims, or just British.

Social scientists now regard the stabilization of ethnic categories as a *political* process in the broadest sense. Ethnic identities are constantly subject to formation and re-formation and to contextual negotiation.

Note too that in the examples I have cited there is no clear distinction made between ethnicity and nationality or sense of national belonging. 'Territoriality' or geographical boundaries are further sources of indeterminacy and negotiation in the formation of ethnicities.

Race, ethnicity, and census classifications

And when 'race' enters the equation the result is a confusing melange of categories, as exhibited in census surveys and also in the following typical 'ethnic group' monitoring form, based on census categories, that patients have to fill in when attending hospitals and other medical facilities, in the British National Health Service:

A. White British

B. White Irish

C. Any other White background (A, B and C to identify Caucasian ethnic backgrounds for medical purposes not nationality)

D. White and Black Caribbean

E. White and Black African

F. White and Asian

G. Any other Mixed background

H. Indian

I. Pakistani

J. Bangladeshi

K. Any other Asian background

L. Black Caribbean

M. Black African

N. Any other Black background

O. Chinese

P. Any other ethnic group

It is not difficult to identify here what is nowadays a chronic confusion in European and North American public discourses and governmental monitoring schemes between *racial* categories such as black, white, and Caucasian, with *national* identities such as Indian and Pakistani, and the further problems created by the 'mixed' classifications that conflate racial (black and white) with geographical classifications such as Asian, Caribbean, and African.

The Asian category also reveals the ambiguities involved in classifying the Chinese, who are allowed a place of their own.

And at least half a century's political struggles by subordinate groups have also left a significant imprint. 'Black', which up to the 1960s was a derogatory label, has been re-appropriated and revalorized by the civil rights and Black Power movements of the USA. The slogan 'Black is Beautiful' empowered populations otherwise also reviled as 'Niggers' and 'Coloureds' in their struggle for civil rights.

In the UK in the 1970s and 1980s, 'black' was adopted by anti-racist movements as part of a relatively successful political strategy to mobilize and unite diverse populations whose origins lay mainly in the Caribbean and South Asia. Amongst other things, it also showed up the racial assumptions of the term 'coloured', in common use even in the 1960s, which took *white*ness as a supposedly *colourless* and invisible norm with which to classify and discriminate against people from the Indian subcontinent and the West Indies.

On the other hand, the increasing educational, economic, political, and cultural fragmentation of the British minority populations in the last part of the 20th century is now also reflected in the need to include separate categories for populations of Indian, Pakistani, Bangladeshi, African, Caribbean, and Chinese origin.

However, note the quasi-scientific manner in which a discredited biological notion of race infiltrates into the heart of the classification and undermines its medical benefits. The idea of 'Caucasian' in Britain is included on medical grounds. But this can be misleading. Illnesses such as cystic fibrosis or sickle-cell anaemia may be more prevalent in some groups that can be identified phenotypically, for example by skin colour. But a great many 'black' and 'white' individuals in the USA and in Britain carry genes from a wide range of so-called racial groups. Thus, statistical information gathered on the basis of categories like 'Caucasian' or 'non-Caucasian' can lead to potentially large groups of blacks, whites, and others being under-represented in health-awareness campaigns and resource distribution for treating particular medical conditions.

Whiteness and ethno-racial census politics in the USA

The category of 'white' in any case poses special problems of its own. In the USA, as I have shown in an earlier chapter, 'whiteness' has never been a simple matter of unambiguous visible difference. Groups like the Irish, Italians, and Jews attained acceptance as 'whites' through political struggle and strategic alliances in which they managed to place themselves apart from African Americans and populations of Chinese origin.

Moreover, as also remarked upon earlier, the definition of 'black' has been seriously warped by the 'one-drop' rule which obviously does not apply to whites – otherwise almost the entire population of black Americans would have to be classified as 'white'!

In the USA, individuals often find themselves having to choose between Euro-American (or white), Asian American, African American, Hispanic (or Latino), and Indigenous Peoples (or Native American).

Now populations of Mexican and Latin American origin constitute the largest minority group in the country. But who really counts as 'Hispanic' is less clear, given the very wide range of linguistic, national, religious, and ethnic backgrounds that can be included. Hispanics have been eligible for favourable treatment under American affirmative action programmes for disadvantaged minorities, but researchers have highlighted the relatively large number of anomalies that have resulted, in so far as many of the Hispanics who have benefited from the programmes have had little connection with Hispanic culture, and in addition have had privileged socio-economic backgrounds.

Especially, the 'whiteness' of American Hispanics remains a matter of ambiguity. The Hispanic classification, after all, is additional to that of 'white'.

Such confusions of colour, culture, and geography, endemic in the definition of race and ethnicity, also make it difficult to decide what is to count as racism, for in some form or another the use of 'racism' necessarily implies that a group is being defined as a 'race' or an individual is being regarded as belonging to a 'race'.

Defining racism: the case of Enoch Powell

By now the success of anti-racist campaigns in the USA and the whole of Western Europe is also reflected in the moral opprobrium attached to the label 'racist'. Hence, in part, the reluctance of citizens and politicians to identify themselves openly as racist.

A quote from Enoch Powell, one of the British politicians most identified with racist views in the last part of the 20th century, gives an indication of how *conventional, classical, or old racism* had come to be defined in the late 19th and most of the 20th centuries.

Asked in 1969 whether he was a racist, Powell replied:

> if by racialist you mean a man who despises a human being because he belongs to another race, or a man who believes that one race is inherently superior to another in civilisation or capability for civilisation, then the answer is emphatically no.

Powell's denial that he was racist, though somewhat disingenuous in ways we shall explore, nevertheless also has a sound and credible basis.

This is evident from the following definition of racism from the eminent British biologist Steven Rose that has been widely accepted by anti-racists too, and which brings together many of the strands of doctrines of race from the 18th century onwards:

> By racism is meant any claim of the natural superiority of one identifiable human population, group or race over another. By 'scientific racism' is meant the attempt to use the language and some of the techniques of science in support of theories or contentions that particular groups or populations are innately inferior to others in terms of intelligence, 'civilisation' or other socially-defined attitudes.

Powell, by jettisoning any claims to natural and innate superiority and inferiority as between human groups, immediately distances himself from forms of thinking that have been taken to be central to racism.

Interestingly, Powell refers not to racism but to 'racialism', and appears to endorse the existence of 'races' as naturally bounded populations. Many scientists and social scientists have argued that any doctrine that accepts that races really exist as naturally bounded populations is thereby racist. On this criterion, Powell would appear to be endorsing at least part of what many commentators would include in a definition of racism.

But it is also the case that by denying any belief in innate superiority and inferiority between races, and also by claiming that there is no warrant for any race despising another, Powell is able to rebut the accusation of racism to a considerable extent.

'Strong/hard racism'

We now have the elements that in combination constitute one common version of what might be called a *strong* or *hard* version of classical, or conventional, or the 'old racism'.

Strong racism can be defined as the belief that separate, distinct, biologically defined races exist; that they can be hierarchically ordered on the basis of innate, and thus unalterable superior and inferior characteristics and abilities; and that hostility is natural between these races.

Each element on its own is a *necessary* but not *sufficient* condition for the identification of 'strong racism'. The racism can be said to be stronger the greater the number of such beliefs it combines.

Other elements are also relevant. Some versions of 'strong racism' may contain additional ideas, for example the view so commonly held in the 19th and early 20th centuries that 'racial mixing' or 'miscegenation' is undesirable because it would lead inevitably to 'degeneration' in the superior race.

There are more issues to confront before a nuanced judgement can be made about the extent of Powell's racism or that of anyone else.

Cultural difference and the 'new racism'

There has been considerable debate since the 1980s, especially in the UK, USA, and France, about a changing relationship between earlier, overt racism and the emergence of a more covert racism which attempts to escape the opprobrium of open racism by omitting issues of *biology* altogether and focusing instead on questions of *culture* and ethnicity.

That is, there has been a growing belief that we have seen the development of a 'new racism'. This has been given a variety of labels: 'cultural racism'; 'neo-racism'; and 'the racism of cultural difference'.

There are good reasons for pursuing the 'new racism' debate before returning to provide more sophisticated and nuanced definitions of racism, which in turn will allow a better understanding of the varieties of contemporary racism.

In particular, a discussion of the complexities introduced by the debates over the new racism will enable us to take a crucial step beyond the present impasse by allowing us to break with the usual practice of attempting to find one tight and restricted definition of racism, although this is what is usually demanded during public debates and in creating anti-discrimination legislation.

Finding criteria which can create strictly separate dichotomies between racism and non-racism, or the racist and the non-racist, has boxed the debates about racism into perspectives which simply fail to illuminate the complexity and variability of the ways in which racism manifests itself. Such attempts tend to occlude the many ways in which racism combines with other, related sorts of beliefs and practices to yield popular cultures and practices of racism which are anything but simply racism. We need to move away from rigid divisions between racism/non-racism and racist/non-racist.

A consideration of some examples, including those referred to in Chapter 1 on 'conundrums', will help us to understand why I think this move is so crucial in freeing the debates from unproductive, entrenched positions which prevent constructive public and scholarly discussion on the subject of racism.

Race, cultural difference, and national identity: turning the tables on racism

If we went on as we are, then by the end of the century there would be 4 million people of the New Commonwealth . . . here. Now that is an awful lot and I think it means that people are really rather afraid that this country might be swamped by people with a different culture. And, you know, the British character has done so much for democracy, for law, and done so much throughout the world, that if there is a fear that it might be swamped, people are going to react and be rather hostile to those coming in.

(Mrs Thatcher, Leader of the Conservative Party, 1978)

This is an interesting and important example of what has been called the new racism. But in what senses is it really racist? Or new?

In answering this question we shall begin to unravel some of the complexities of contemporary discourses on race. And, thereby, the difficulties of assigning clear cut labels such as 'racist' and 'non-racist' to individuals or individual statements.

Arguably, Mrs Thatcher's remarks are not racist in the following respects. They make no direct reference to 'race' and nor to any 'racial' marker strongly associated with past racism, like skin colour, size of brain or shape of nose. Indeed, the statements appear to be devoid of all biological referents and therefore seem very far from any form of what I have dubbed classical or 19th- and first-half-of-the-20th-century racism.

Nor is there an obvious reference to superiority and inferiority of peoples, especially with an underlying biological determinism, a staple of classical racism. Instead, and this in particular is what is supposedly new, the emphasis is on cultural difference and the genuine fears of ordinary citizens that their national character and, by implication, way of life may be in danger of being overwhelmed and marginalized.

However, note the strong contrast between British national culture and the character of outsiders from countries populated by non-white peoples. The 'New Commonwealth', in British political culture, has always functioned in a colour-coded manner by being contrasted with the predominantly white Old Commonwealth of Australia, New Zealand, and Canada.

Moreover, Mrs Thatcher singles out the British nation as a unique cultural formation. The racial significance of this reference is crucial. Historically, as we have seen, the concepts of nation and race have constantly been elided since the 18th century. Ideas of the 'nation' have consistently combined cultural, territorial, and biological proto-racial elements. Notions of distinct Anglo-Saxon, Germanic, Gallic, Slavic, and other racial cultures have strongly influenced ideas of unique British, German, French, and Russian national characteristics.

And colour and culture are strongly intertwined by chains of association in Mrs Thatcher's remarks. There is a strong implication that the brown and black New Commonwealth peoples lack commitment to democratic values and the rule of law. Moreover, they are portrayed as not having made a contribution to world history and global cultural achievements.

Thus connotations of biological, colour-based, nationally bounded cultural superiority and inferiority are strongly carried by the suggestion that democracy, the rule of law, and other contributions to global civilization have been made by British, and generally white – not 'New Commonwealth' – peoples.

Of course the white/non-white division and its association with democracy and other features is achieved by presenting a highly compressed and selective history of British imperialism in which brutal dispossession of land and resources, slavery, exploitation and myriad massacres of non-white 'natives' in the Caribbean, Africa, and the Indian subcontinent are whitewashed out of the picture. Moreover, the fact that independent status was granted to the non-white colonies (and the USA) only after violent struggle, and democracy hastily and ineffectually installed prior to a swift exit is also ignored. As is the suppression of democracy by white minority regimes of the time, such as Southern Rhodesia (Zimbabwe) and apartheid South Africa.

The extent to which Mrs Thatcher's claims are part of a deliberate, intentional obfuscation to hide possible racism is not easy to decipher, and this sort of question bedevils discussion of racism. I provide more detailed elaboration on this issue of intentionality later.

While the passage reproduced above manages to avoid explicit reference to 'race', Mrs Thatcher's attachment to the idea of race is openly exhibited in her rallying cry in 1982 for support for war with Argentina over the Falkland Islands, a sentiment immediately echoed in *The Times* newspaper:

> The people of the Falkland Islands, like the people of the United Kingdom, are an island race. Their way of life is British; their allegiance is to the Crown.
>
> (Mrs Thatcher, House of Commons, 3 April 1982)

> We are an island race, and the focus of attack is one of our islands, inhabited by islanders.
>
> (*The Times*, 5 April 1982)

These remarks are typical examples of the manner in which in more recent periods race, nation and culture ('way of life') can create effective chains of association.

Seen in this context, it is clear that it is not possible to understand the way in which race now operates by looking only at single statements in isolation and deciding whether they are racist or not. Race operates in a whole variety of guises and with a myriad taken for granted assumptions that have become embedded in public and private cultures in which ideas of nation, ethnicity, 'way of life' and other concepts have sometimes strong, sometimes less intense racial connotations. The actual racism of statements such as those by Mrs Thatcher is a matter of complex and always debatable judgement.

How 'race' can trump 'culture'

The convenient way in which emphases can shift between various aspects of biology (or race) and nation or (culture) was evident at the time of these 1980s British debates over immigration by use of the notion of 'stock', suggesting that people of Asian and African Caribbean origin were not only culturally different but different from genuine British people who were regarded as being of Anglo-Saxon stock. Apart from excluding people of Jewish and Irish origin, this also had the unintended consequence of ignoring the huge impact of the 1066 Norman Conquest and settling of Britain, to mention just one of many movements of people into Britain.

'Anglo-Saxon' still functions as a shorthand descriptor for British peoples and institutions, creating a strong biological undercurrent for narratives of who does and does not legitimately belong to the nation.

This is the type of underlying assumption which allowed Enoch Powell to claim that 'the West Indian does not by being born in England, become an Englishman. In law, he becomes a United Kingdom citizen by birth; *in fact he is a West Indian or an Asian still*' (emphasis added), or enabled the British comedian Bernard Manning to insist on several occasions that just as a dog does not become a horse simply by being born in a stable, so Asians and blacks do not become English by being born in England. That dogs and horses are different species makes this sort of statement, supposedly jokingly, a very strong form of biologically based racism. This chillingly recalls the claim by Goebbels, one of Hitler's key henchman, that 'The fact that the Jew lives among us is no proof that he belongs with us, just as a flea does not become a domestic animal because it lives in the house.'

That the 'new racism' co-exists with and can so easily slip into hard biological conceptions of stock and even species should alert us to the fact that it is easy to exaggerate the divide between an 'old' biological racism and a 'new' cultural racism. While taboos against biologically based conceptions have become stronger and classical racial arguments have lost scientific credibility, they both continue an underground existence and are always available as resources to be drawn upon in arguments over immigration, national belonging and citizenship.

The immigrant as the 'real racist'

If there are cases of race trumping culture when necessary, culture can trump race in the most unexpected ways. This is evident in arguments common in the 1980s (and now revived in a different form) that the real racists are not indigenous whites, but the black and Asian immigrants who insist on keeping alive a wide range of their own ways of life while still wanting to claim full rights as British citizens and turning whites into 'second-class citizens'.

In other words, immigrants (and the reference here is primarily to non-whites) who refuse to assimilate into the host British culture, including wanting to marry within their own ethnic minority communities, are regarded as racist towards Britons and British national culture.

Also, this assertion is made at the same time as the arguments, exemplified by those of Powell, Manning and others, that being born in this country only entitles the immigrant to legal status as citizens, not entry into Englishness or Britishness. Thus the hapless black and Asian immigrants are placed in a 'Catch 22' situation, condemned for not assimilating but simultaneously said to be not capable of assimilation by being of different 'stock'.

These arguments have not been restricted to Britain. A complex and flexible 'new racism' has been a prominent feature of debates in France and other European nation-states. In France similar ideas were propagated in the 1980s by the conservative GRECE (Groupement de Recherche et d'Etudes pour la Civilisation

Europeenne) and the neo-liberal Le Club de l'Horlogie, a group of businessmen, civil servants and intellectuals. In response, French sociologists have distinguished between an old racism of *inegalitarianism* that treated non-whites as inferior, and a post-colonialist racism of (cultural) *differentialism* which supports policies of excluding non-white minorities on the grounds that their cultures are incompatible with the French national culture or way of life.

However, it is necessary again to see that these forms of proposed exclusion contain various biological elements. France was unique amongst the countries of Western Europe in the 1980s and early 1990s in having a 'new racism' that was much more closely allied to an extreme-right, neo-fascist movement (the National Front led by Jean Marie Le Pen), a situation more common in Europe now, as we shall see. But there is an essential continuity between Le Pen's cultural defence of French national identity and the assumptions underlying the views of Powell.

Le Pen, like Powell and others in Britain, has always buttressed his nationalism with biological notions of the 'naturalness' of preferring one's own kind, thus treating the nation as a biological as well as cultural entity. As Le Pen put it in a famous proclamation, 'I prefer my daughters to my nieces and my nieces to my neighbours, like everyone else . . . all men are the same'.

This makes a complex combination of biological and cultural features seem just simple 'common sense', a form of association also very prevalent in the debates in the UK. Opposition to the argument is made to seem ridiculous and contrary to what 'everyone knows to be obviously true'. An argument and policies based on 'common sense' can thus have consequences which have fairly obvious racial elements and can be legitimately regarded as *racist* in some form, serving to exclude 'Arabs', Africans and Asians as inevitably and forever outside the nation.

'It's only human nature': the defence of territory and national identity

Since the 1980s another twist has been added to this complex set of manoeuvres to exclude non-white citizens from properly belonging to the nation.

A new lease of life has been given to the argument that it is not racist to attempt to prevent outsiders from settling in one's own country. The drawing of group boundaries and the defence of territory and identity are posited as natural human responses. As Powell put it, 'An instinct to preserve an identity and defend a territory is one of the deepest and strongest implanted in mankind' (9 June 1969).

At the time, and even more so since, these claims have been bolstered by drawing upon the newer disciplines of sociobiology and evolutionary psychology and are discussed later.

For the present note three consequences of such arguments. Firstly, the argument from *group* identity is conflated with the idea that *nations* are natural entities which humans will instinctively defend. Secondly, it implies that *national* animosities and hostility towards foreigners are only *natural*. And thirdly, that immigrants should only move to countries to which they can belong 'naturally'.

In effect the argument then becomes that the 'natural' home of black and Asian immigrants cannot possibly be a white nation-state such as Britain. This chain of reasoning ends up with the conclusion that it is unfair on both non-white immigrants and the white indigenous population that blacks and Asians should settle in Britain. It is contrary to 'nature'.

Hence biology re-enters the cultural arena to bolster what then becomes an unambiguously racist argument that it is contrary to *nature* that white, black and Asian populations can ever live harmoniously.

In fact, arguments of the sort made by Le Pen (and Powell) are based on selective and simplistic narratives that marginalize internal divisions within families as well as nations, and allow the family as a biological entity to function as a surrogate for nation, 'race' and whiteness. The French tradition of secularism is often simultaneously exploited by that country's right to label 'Arab', mainly North African immigrants from France's former colonies, as the *real* racists, for resisting complete assimilation into a supposedly ethnically neutral, civic, liberal, mainstream culture, and especially for wanting a public role for Islam in a manner contrary to the secularist tradition.

Debates about the role of religion – especially Islam – in public life have now taken a new turn throughout Europe.

'Cultural racism'

If a purely cultural or religious argument devoid of any reference to biological relations is made, can it be called 'racist' without stretching the meaning of the label to a point where it becomes too wide to be useful as anything but a rhetorical ploy?

In principle, a form of group identification or classification that relies only on criteria such as mode of dress, language, customs, and religion, to name but a few, might more properly be subsumed under the ideas of *ethnicism* or *ethnocentrism* rather than having any connotations of 'race', and may be said to border on *xenophobia* if the criteria include membership of national groups and contain elements of hostility to 'foreigners' and non-nationals.

In practice, though, *cultural* demarcations are often drawn and used in a form that *naturalizes* them by implying that they are more or less *immutable*. Thus the supposed avariciousness of Jews, the alleged aggressiveness of Africans and African Americans, the criminality of Afro-Caribbeans or the slyness of 'Orientals', become traits that are invariably attached to these groups over extremely long periods of time. The descriptions may then be drawn upon as part of a common-sense vocabulary of stereotypes that blur any strict distinction between culture and biology.

Thus the slippage into the idea of Jews as a 'race' *and* religious group is easily made via the bridging concept of an almost invariable trait of monetary greed, and where the exception 'only proves the rule', thus making the statement immune to empirical counter-cases.

The argument I am making about the way social features are naturalized may be put in more technical social scientific terms by referring to the concept of *essentialism*. That is, what allows cultural traits and biological classifications to operate together as part of an almost seamless framework is the notion of an unchanging 'essence' that underlies the superficial differences of historical time and place.

In *this* sense it is possible to talk of 'cultural racism' despite the fact that strictly speaking modern ideas of race have always had one or other biological foundation. To argue, as many do, that there has to be an explicit reference to biological features such as shape of nose or skin colour or genetic inheritance if a proposition is to be described as racist is strictly speaking accurate. But it misses the point that generalizations, stereotypes, and other forms of cultural essentialism rest and draw upon a wider reservoir of concepts that are in circulation in popular and public culture. Thus, the racist elements of any particular proposition can only be judged by understanding the general context of public and private discourses in which ethnicity, national identifications, and race coexist in blurred and overlapping forms without clear demarcations.

Racisms

The complex and multilayered manner in which the category of 'race' now functions in the public life and interpersonal relations of nation-states has led many commentators to argue that it is necessary to speak not just of a single racism, but always to think about racism*s* in the plural.

Public statements that have more recently been the subject of dispute about their racism – as we shall see for the case of religion too – may vary considerably in the biological and or cultural features they refer to. Some may focus partly on physiological characteristics such as skin colour or shape of eyes – Prince Phillip famously and controversially warned British people he met on a visit to China to beware of becoming 'slitty-eyed' if they stayed too long – but the biological aspects vary considerably, as will the cultural attributes, including supposed general inferiority and superiority, or specific degree of capacity for 'civilization' and intellectual and technological achievement. To stay with the notorious Prince Phillip, he once also referred to what he regarded as the lamentable state of wiring in a British public building as 'Indian'.

These instances illustrate that the recommendation to always understand the plurality of racisms is well taken, although this is not necessarily to endorse the view that Prince Philip's comments were unambiguously racist anyway. In any case, it is necessary to recognize that it is fruitless to attempt and impossible to provide some sort of definitive classification of different types of racism. Racist beliefs may take a different form whether being applied to whites, Asians, blacks, or Jews, and depending on the degree to which are sexualized and combined with ideas of nationality.

Racialization and racism

It is in the context of difficulties of this type that the concept of *racialization* has become more common in social scientific research. This acknowledges that propositions, insults, and more elaborate doctrines are liable to vary in the degree to which they contain the elements of what I have referred to as 'strong' or 'hard' racism. Exploring the degree to which propositions rest on biological or physiological divisions between populations, and the extent to which notions of innate superiority and inferiority are overtly or covertly included, for example, allow a judgement to be made of the *degree* of racialization and racism.

The concept of racialization moves research and political argument away from the unproductive debates about whether any particular individuals, propositions, claims, and doctrines are simply 'racist' or 'non-racist'. Instead, the field is opened up to more useful analyses of the different mixes of biological and cultural connotations of difference, superiority and inferiority that emerge in public and private statements, conversations, jokes, and so forth.

The popularity of the concept of 'racialization' in recent social scientific research thus rests on the acknowledgement that the simple label racism/racist obscures the fact that there is in fact a whole spectrum of views from strict biological determinism – of the type that 'blacks are less intelligent and this is because of their genetic inheritance' – to very confused and loose mixes of cultural stereotypes which may not contain any specific biological markers at all: 'Indian electrical wiring is a joke' or 'Of course he's miserly, he is Jewish/Scottish'.

Racialization also does not imply that those subjected to it are necessary regarded as inferior. Thus it also encompasses the not uncommon notions of the innate cleverness of Jews or Japanese. And the application of covert quotas in the past against the admission of these groups for fear of their domination of places at prestigious American universities was no less racist for being based on the supposed superiority of populations of Jewish and Japanese origin.

Religious racism? The case of Islamophobia

In the wake of the attacks on the Twin Towers in New York on 11 September 2001 and the rise of militant or radical Islamism in various parts of the world in the last part of the 20th and the early part of the 21st century, it has increasingly been argued that a new fear, 'Islamophobia', has gripped the Western world and is reflected in general suspicion, physical attacks against mosques and Muslim individuals, and discriminatory behaviour by state agencies especially the police against Muslim communities. Statistical evidence certainly bears out that overt discrimination of all types against Muslims living in Europe and the USA has shown an often dramatic increase.

Islamophobia is said to draw upon historical associations relating to the long-standing hostility and military conflicts that occurred in medieval and early modern Europe, culminating in the Crusades and the dramatic defeat of Islamic power in Spain in 1492. The use by the American President George Bush of the idea of a 'crusade' against Islamic radicals, amongst a host of other statements and publications against Islam – for example, a whole spate of books in Italy and France criticizing the illiberality, backwardness, and misogyny of 'fundamentalist' Islam and comparing it unfavourably with Christianity – have lent support to the notion of a new Islamophobia in the West.

This hostility to Islam has often been described as a form of *racism*. How credible is the equation between Islamophobia and racism?

Two problems with the idea of Islamophobia should be noted in passing. Firstly, the idea of 'phobia' is unhelpful, because of its implications of mental illness and pathology, an issue that is discussed later. Secondly, as the political scientist Fred Halliday has quite rightly pointed out, the term is too broad and encompasses such a large range of views and practices that it impedes nuanced understanding of the phenomenon.

Whether Islamophobia can be regarded as a form of *racism*, though, is worth pursuing briefly. Given that Muslims globally have all shades of skin colour, ethnicity, and nationality, it is difficult to argue in any straightforward way that even if Islamophobia exists, it is a form of racism. The use of the notion of *racialization*, rather than plunging the discussion straight into a stark choice between racism/non-racism, can be helpful.

Consider one popular argument against Turkey's membership of the European Union, that because Turkey, although not a theocratic state, has a majority Muslim population it can never be properly integrated with European culture. Arguably the issue is racialized by the predominant European view of Turks as also non-white, but the degree to which this attitude to Islam is a form of *racism* would require the arguments to be unpacked. For example, to what extent is this lack of assimilability regarded as relatively permanent, thus naturalizing and essentializing Islam and Muslims? And are the religion and its followers regarded as generally inferior or uncivilized? Such judgements are often implicit, but in some contexts and publications are more overtly made. Thus, the argument around Islam in the context of Turkey is not necessarily racist. It may be more or less so, or not at all.

In the UK, the extreme-right British National Party leaders have been secretly filmed at their meetings where their speeches have explicitly conflated 'Muslims' and 'Asians' as rapists of vulnerable white teenagers. The degree of racism and the consciousness of intention here is arguably much clearer than in most opinions against Turkey's membership of the European Union. A legal prosecution of two leaders of the BNP on the grounds of 'inciting racial hatred' has so far been unsuccessful. The question of Islam is also central to the case as the BNP leader Nick Griffin is distinctly heard denouncing the religion as wicked and evil, as allowing the rape of infidel women, and therefore is regarded by him as a crucial element in the Asians' racist behaviour against white women. The intertwining of racism and the sexuality of immigrants and foreigners that is evident here is of course a long-standing theme in racist beliefs.

Islamophobia and racism: the case of Kilroy-Silk

Islamophobia's possible racism was also an issue in the Kilroy-Silk affair mentioned in the first chapter. While this example may seem too limited by its context, it allows an exploration of issues relevant to other instances which are likely to recur.

What is striking about the British broadcaster's comments in his newspaper column is the way in which there is an indiscriminate conflation between religion and race, Islam and Arabs. His article in the *Sunday Express* of 4 January 2004 was entitled 'We Owe Arabs Nothing'. It castigated 'Arabs', Muslims, and Islam for making no contribution to real civilization. 'They' had only given 'us' oil, 'suicide bombers, limb amputators and women oppressors'.

'Arab' regimes are labelled barbarous, and in a by-line in bold, Kilroy-Silk concludes that it is obvious that 'not all cultures are morally equal'. This is just a sample of the remarks in the article.

In response to critics of Kilroy-Silk, his morning television show was taken off the air by the BBC, and the country became embroiled in yet another debate about the meaning of racism and the 'political correctness' to which he had supposedly fallen victim.

But how *racist* were his remarks in the light of the discussion provided in this book?

In recklessly generalizing about all 'Arabs' – and he even includes Iran, not an 'Arab' nation, in his remarks – and denouncing them for lack of civilization, Kilroy-Silk has certainly strayed into racist territory. 'Arab' is a geo-linguistic, proto-racial category. By labelling all Arabs uncivilized, as he does in effect, Kilroy-Silk is repeating a classic racist move, treating 'them' *all* – Arab nations and individuals – as inferior to 'us' ('we', by strong implication, are all whites, Christians, Europeans, and Westerners).

It is not unreasonable to relate his remarks to some sort of 'Islamophobia' despite the problematic nature of this term, and to use his comments to illustrate how in everyday usage religious groups are racialized to create a field of debate in which 'race', culture, religion, and political regimes get confusingly conflated. 'Islamophobia' or any other kind of hostility to Islam and Muslims is not *necessarily* racist, but in many contexts can take a *relatively* 'strong' or 'hard' racist form as it *appears* to do in the case of Kilroy-Silk.

If the *remarks* are broadly within the terrain of racism does that mean that it is fair to call Kilroy-Silk a racist? This may appear to be the same issue but, despite overlaps, should be regarded as an analytically distinct question, to do with racist *identity*, as we shall see.

Before considering the question of racist identities, however, it is necessary to discuss another difficult issue raised by the Kilroy-Silk affair: the question of *intention* in judging the racism of an action, including the making of potentially racist comments.

Words, intentions, and actions

In July 2004 the British Crown Prosecution Service decided not to charge Kilroy-Silk with the offence of 'incitement to racial hatred' or any other under the Race Relations legislation. The CPS concluded that Kilroy-Silk's remarks against Arabs and Muslims were not 'intentionally insulting'. Indeed, Kilroy-Silk had apologized for the remarks, claiming in the next day's *Daily Express* that he had never intended to insult the world's 200 million Arabs' and that he had 'aimed his criticism at a number of repressive, autocratic governments in the Middle East and the extremists they sheltered'. In the *Sunday Express* a week after the original article, he pointed out: 'I didn't intend to say that all Arabs are uncivilized because clearly I don't believe that. That's stupid. That's nonsense.'

The question of whether racism is an *intended* or *unintended* aspect of any particular statement or utterance is clearly important, especially in the legal context such as the issue of Kilroy-Silk's guilt or otherwise.

Racist utterances do not prove that the person or group making them intended the remarks to be understood as racist and would be hurtful in that specific manner. Nor do they mean that that person or group will necessarily and automatically carry out *other* kinds of discriminatory practices or has done so in the past.

This is not simply a matter of academic or research interest. It can become a vital issue when judgements are being made about racist behaviour. A remarkable incident that emerged in the trial of the white youths accused of the racist murder of the black teenager Stephen Lawrence in 1993 in London aptly and tragically illustrates the importance and often intractability of this issue.

In order to gather evidence against the five white youths suspected of having committed the murder, police secretly filmed the suspects at home. The footage shows the young men shouting racist obscenities and play-acting with knives. But the film was not used as evidence. It would have been easy for the youths to argue in court, as they had done publicly, that they were only 'fooling around' or 'messing about', and that the incidents reveal nothing about their intentions or their guilt in actually committing the murder of

Stephen Lawrence. The youths have never been convicted of the murder of Stephen Lawrence.

The issue of the relationship between speech acts and other forms of discriminatory behaviour remains problematic, and inferences have to be made with care and close attention to context and other behaviour. What might seem plausible at a common-sense level does not necessarily convince when judgements of proof beyond reasonable doubt have to be made.

Chapter 7

Racist identities: ambivalence, contradiction, and commitment

Let us begin with Kilroy-Silk, again. I expressed the judgement above that his remarks on 'Arabs' constituted a relatively strong form of racialization, and thereby had already entered the terrain of racism by using some of its key elements. Furthermore, his cavalier description of Arabs as inferior meant that the charge of racism has further plausibility, although I must stress that this is not the same as labelling him a racist in some absolute, definitive sense.

In support of Kilroy-Silk, he and others cited the frequent appearance of British ethnic minority individuals on his breakfast television show and the fact that he employed a black driver.

But are we entitled to conclude that Kilroy-Silk is therefore not racist? This is where his *identity* as a racist – and that of others who make such remarks or perform other acts with a strong element of racialization – becomes an issue.

Understanding identities

But what constitutes an identity? In recent years the social sciences have been engulfed by significant debates and new thinking on this subject. In what follows, I will draw out in abbreviated form what I regard to be the most salient themes that can help us understand issues relevant to the question of racist identities.

Firstly, an individual or group identity is only partly a matter of *self*-identification. Identities are also assigned by others or created by the state and civic institutions. Census categories and other social surveys which box people into groups such as white, black, 'mixed', Christian, Muslim, and so forth are a powerful source of such identificatory labels.

Secondly, identities usually imply and rely on the *recognition of difference*. Being American, black, female, young, and so forth are in part possible because others can be and are classified as Chinese, white, male, and old. Therefore, drawing boundaries around characteristics of 'sameness', and thus belonging, necessarily involves practices of exclusion and the creation of identities of non-belonging for others.

The fact that any identity also requires identifying what it is not, means that any identity is potentially open to being threatened and destabilized by identities that are being denied. For example, male identity can only be sustained by identification with certain norms of masculinity, but given the myriad commonalities between men and women, and the fact that conceptions of masculinity and femininity are subject to historical change, male behaviour and masculine identity characterized by 'toughness', 'independence', aversion to childcare, and so forth are always open to being subverted by 'tenderness' and softness, open display of emotions or affection, commitment to childcare, and so forth. It is important to emphasize that the necessity of difference does not imply the necessity of 'prejudice', 'threat', and hostility. As Billig has pointed out in a seminal contribution, the categorization and classification of others by individuals and groups is a complex and variable process. One significant point is that *generalizations* coexist with attention to *particulars*, so generalized hostility is not an automatic product of individual and group attempts at classifying the surrounding social world. As anthropological evidence, summarized, for example, by Elizabeth Cashden, shows, loyalty to one's own group is not automatically accompanied by hostility to members of other groups. Thus tolerance, co-operation, and openness are as likely outcomes of the creation of categories and identities as are 'prejudice' and hostility.

Thirdly, the drawing of boundaries and the creation of identities emerge out of a *process* in which individuals have to decide and assert who they are in *negotiation* with other identity-assigning agents such as their families, the religious communities into which they may be born, the education system which grades and labels them in various ways, and local and national state regulations, including race relations legislation. Thus, identities are the outcome of *processes* of *power relations* and are located in *structures of authority*.

Fourthly, *identities* as bounded entities *are not permanently fixed*. The transformation of those labelled as 'niggers' into 'coloured', and thence to 'black' and 'African American', is an obvious and telling case in point of changes in *self*-identification as part of organized, political campaigning to change *public* identities through their recognition and location in public structures of power and authority. But individual identities, including *racist* identities, are also relatively provisional and open to transformation. They are not completely frozen in time and space.

The above examples highlight an important lesson from current debates on identity. It is more important to frame our thinking about identity in terms of *processes of identification*.

Fifthly, identities always involve *multiplicity*. Individuals have multiple roles and a variety of 'subject positions' pertaining to different roles and identifications. A woman may be wife, sister, daughter, and a militant feminist, setting up diverse identifications and the potential for opening up to a variety of other individuals in different circumstances.

Sixthly, identities, therefore, are rarely coherent and integrated.

They are prone to *inconsistency* and *contradiction*, depending on the context. Boys and men may behave in a tough, 'macho' style when with other males, in schools and workplaces, but may display softer, supposedly more 'feminine' aspects at home with their own children, spouses, and younger siblings.

One reason that identities lack coherence is because societies tend to have potentially contradictory moral principles embedded in their public cultures. Social psychologists such as Mike Billig have thus argued that individuals constantly find themselves in situations where they are placed in *dilemmas* as to how they should behave, and they can and do choose to act differently and inconsistently at different times or places.

For instance, liberal Western societies contain powerful legitimations of inequalities in resources between individuals, and ideas about the inferiority of women or different ethnic groups, but at the same time have strongly embedded egalitarian traditions and legislative measures that sanction equal rights, fair treatment, and taboos against racism. We should also bear in mind Katz's insight, referred to in my discussion of the Holocaust, that individuals can compartmentalize different expectations into separate moral spheres, allowing them to behave in accordance with different ethical rules in different contexts, for example as between the concentration camp and the home.

Psychoanalytic perspectives have also had some influence on recent conceptions of identity, leading to the conclusion that individuals are *de-centred* in the sense of having their behaviour influenced by unconscious motivations, projections of inner fears and bad feelings about the self onto others, and so forth. In thus not being fully self-aware and fully knowledgeable about their own inner selves, individuals may behave inconsistently and in a contradictory manner.

Psychoanalytic, dilemmatic, and other forms of de-centring discussed above also make it possible to grasp the way in which contradictory pressures and unconscious motivations may generate *ambivalence* and *contradiction* when it comes to relationships with others. In my view, this is a point of considerable significance in understanding racism, as we shall see.

In general, an important conclusion from psychoanalytic, and the other conceptions of identity discussed above, is that individual identities are always subject to unconscious anxieties, fears, and continuous, vague, or more focused insecurities, which can be exacerbated in times of rapid change or in encounters with strangers. This has obvious implications for the exacerbation of racism against immigrants and ethnic minorities in times of intense globalization and the rapid transformation of communities and locales.

Finally, it is important to grasp that *group* or social identities also lack inner coherence. Therefore individuals who belong to a particular group are faced with different conceptions of what membership of the group really means for their identity. 'Woman', for instance, is not a unified category. There are middle-class and working-class women, black and white, Chinese and American, British Pakistani and British African Caribbean, mothers and singletons, sisters and daughters, heterosexual or lesbian, to take some of the most obvious social divisions between women with different and potentially contradictory implications for self-identity and individual action, and collective identity and group action.

Putting this final point in more social scientific terms, it is important to be vigilant against the *essentialization* of collective categories and identities. It is impossible to find a single 'essence' or core in a collective identity. There is no essential, singular way in which to be a man, woman, teenager, American, or African. *Or racist.*

The racism of racist identities

These transformations in the general understanding of identities, as I have also argued in *Racism, Modernity and Identity* (1994), can throw considerable light on the conundrums and controversies generated by examples of possibly racist behaviour.

Continuing with the case of Kilroy-Silk, note, in addition to his newspaper piece on Arabs, some other remarks attributed to him. Amongst them have been the following. 'The orgy of thieving in Iraq has more to do with the character of the people than the absence of restraining troops.' On the Irish, he has been quoted as describing them as 'peasants, priests and pixies'. On immigration: 'Why imply the increase in promiscuity is due to promiscuity among the young, indigenous population when it is entirely due to immigration?' In addition, his membership of the United Kingdom Independence Party, and subsequently his attempt to set up his own version of this movement, displays a strong streak of nationalism and hostility to closer ties with other nations, even white ones.

What the statements and behaviour display is a strongly racialized identity that is combined with hostility to other nations and ethnicities and a tendency to view them stereotypically and simplistically as possessing innate, unattractive characteristics. The evidence points to an individual who has a tendency to view others relatively consistently through a racialized framework. There is even a tendency to project unacceptable (sexual) behaviour entirely on to racialized minorities as opposed to 'the indigenous population', a phrase that also appears to betray a tendency to not offer recognition to the belongingness of ethnic minorities to the British nation.

Without a thorough study of Kilroy-Silk's identifications and behaviour, any judgement inevitably has to be tentative. However, on a spectrum or continuum of non-racism to racism, publicly available evidence appears to reveal more elements of a racist identity than a non-racist identity. Employment of a black driver, a relatively lowly occupation, hardly constitutes mitigation.

This brings us back to the case of the football commentator Ron Atkinson, also mentioned in Chapter 1, 'Conundrums', which seems to be more complex than that of Kilroy-Silk. At a point when Atkinson believed that the microphone was switched off he described a black footballer as 'a fucking lazy thick nigger'. On the face of it, so to speak, the remarks have obvious racist connotations, reproducing a widespread stereotype of black laziness, repeating a common insulting judgement about black intelligence, and using the word 'nigger', which has long been regarded as an unacceptable, derogatory reference to black people.

Atkinson promptly apologized for the remarks, claimed that he was not a racist, but resigned. This was not the end of the matter. Atkinson was also reputed to be someone who had been a pioneer in promoting black football talent, and some black footballers came out publicly in support of Atkinson. Other black footballers, however, said that Atkinson was well known for racially abusing black footballers, and they claimed to have personal experiences of such abuse.

What is one to make of Atkinson's alleged racism? Did the unguarded comments reveal his *real* views, camouflaged by support for black players which could be seen simply as a cynical strategy for opportunistically taking advantage of potential skills?

On the basis of what I have said about the nature of personal and social identities in general, and judging on the basis of limited information about him we would be justified in concluding that Atkinson, like many others, has *contradictory* and *ambivalent* responses to black people. He is neither really only a racist nor really a non-racist. Like most white people in Britain, he has culturally absorbed both sorts of views, and his response to any particular black person depends on the context and circumstances in which he is interacting with the black individuals.

Atkinson-type responses can be better understood in the light of my earlier comments on the multiplicity of identities of individuals as well as the resulting de-centredness of their subjectivity such that individuals are not always fully knowledgeable about the layers of identification in their makeup, nor in control of their responses, so that they may end up behaving in a manner they abhor and have long tried to avoid.

A couple of striking illustrations of this sort of 'de-centredness' can be found in incidents reported from the USA. The slips of the tongue which resulted in the secretary of state Condoleezza Rice being referred to as a 'coon' in March 2006, when a talk show host on radio was trying to use the word 'coup', and 'coon' (nearly) slipping out when another radio broadcaster was talking about Martin Luther King in 2005, which resulted in his also being sacked, appear to be graphic examples of a racist vocabulary and perception unconsciously embedded in otherwise liberal individuals and emerging into conscious utterance without warning and with serious consequences for the speakers.

If this interpretation of such incidents is accepted, as I think it should, it marks a radical departure from the conventional impasse in which so many accusations of racism end up, with denials, counter-accusations, anger, and a sense of unfair treatment on both sides. The important thing when issues of this kind arise is not simply to try and come to a definite judgement of 'guilt', although this is obviously required in legal contexts, but to learn from it how individuals, in the arena of 'race' relations and elsewhere are continuously juggling with a variety of identities and narratives, a range of 'scripts' and languages in making sense of situations and responding to them, and understand why it is necessary to engage in a constant and constructive public dialogue about how our responses can break out of grids and frameworks that rely on simplistic accusations of racism and equally simplistic ideas of non-racist identities. The labelling of an action, including an utterance, as 'racist' should be the beginning of a dialogue and enquiry, not the prelude to a round of polarized shouting matches from entrenched positions. Discussion of the nature and multidimensional character of racism should be part of an ongoing public conversation. Combating and unravelling racisms are part of a continuous, long-term project. And it should be democratic, not authoritarian, in form.

Amongst other things, we must always be on guard not to read off a rigid, highly committed racist identity from the fact of voting for a racist party. This became clear in earlier discussions of Germans who voted for the Nazi Party, and has implications for understanding the widely varying commitments to racism amongst those who vote for extreme right parties today.

However, three possible traps should be avoided. Firstly, in the case of racist identities, not everything is always possible. It *is* possible to arrive at provisional judgements about the relative strength of racist identifications in individuals who have behaved in an ostensibly racist manner. For example, on the information available publicly, it is possible to conclude that Kilroy-Silk has a stronger and more consistent racialized identity than Atkinson. But this does not mean that he is going to behave in a racist manner to all individuals or will demean all ethnic minority cultures at all times. There are complex and variable relationships between racist acts in particular contexts, the holding of well-worked-out or vague, 'common-sense' racist beliefs which combine race, nation, ethnicity, and 'way of life', and having strong or weak, consistent or ambivalent and contradictory racist identities.

Secondly, individuals may respond differently to different racialized groups. Take another case from 'Conundrums', David Tovey who had married a Chinese woman, lived with another of Jamaican origin, but was planning violent racist attacks against British Asians (referring to them as 'Pakis' and 'niggers'), especially Muslims. This, amongst a host of cases, illustrates my earlier point about the folly of essentializing racist identities. There is no singular way of being racist.

Finally, it is important to bear in mind that although racist views are often impervious to 'rational' counter-argument and evidence, even those who appear to have shown a strong commitment to racism may change their minds when confronted by different evidence. As an example, one can cite the woman who won a seat for the ultra-right British National Party in local elections in the town of Burnley, having campaigned for the BNP because she believed the Party's claims that the local council had been biased in favour of local Asians in relation to allocation of resources, but who resigned from office in February 2004 after seeing official accounts of how resources had been distributed which showed that the council had in fact acted fairly. To have labelled the woman 'racist' without qualification would have been to miss the important possibility of seeing her as she was, a reflective actor open to counter-evidence and counter-argument galvanized into political activism by grievances she believed at the time.

And of course, we should never forget that Wilhelm Marr, pioneer of modern anti-Semitism, married Jewish women and eventually recanted and begged forgiveness from the Jewish people.

How much racism? Ambivalence and contradiction in black–white relations in the USA

The more complex approach to understanding racism and racist identities I am advocating is supported by a substantial body of social science research. In particular, research bears out the interpretation that many of those whose identities appear to be solidly racist also have views and attitudes, and engage in behaviour that is non-racist. There is much inconsistency and contradiction in white American views of African Americans, for example, which the white individuals live with, deploying a range of conscious, semi-conscious, and unconscious strategies and defence mechanisms to shore up particular views in specific contexts.

Ambivalence, in other words, is as much a characteristic as simple racism in the views of those who might be simply dismissed as racist. The issue of white ambivalence towards African Americans is a key theme of social psychologist Paul Wachtel's excellent discussion in *Race in the Mind of America* (1999).

And in combination with ambivalence, the idea of *racialization* as an uneven, variable, multidimensional, and 'incomplete' phenomenon is more useful than a simplistic differentiation between racists and non-racists.

Of course, this makes it particularly difficult to arrive at blanket and definitive judgements about the degree of racism in American society (and elsewhere), or the character and extent of changes in racism. Although there is general agreement amongst American researchers that there has been a decline in covert expressions of racist belief, there is considerable disagreement about its significance. Many claim that any reduction in racism as measured in attitude surveys is partly at least a consequence of awareness on the part of interviewees and respondents that racism has become increasingly culturally unacceptable in America. They therefore disguise their real views, and thus social scientific and public opinion surveys underestimate the real degree of racism against African Americans.

Inevitably, researchers have tried ingenious methods to reveal the real views of American whites. Sometimes participants are attached to equipment which they are led to believe monitors physiological reactions which will demonstrate their real views. Researchers argue that in such circumstances, where respondents think that their real views will be exposed, the results show higher levels of negative views of blacks.

On the other hand, widely discussed research by the political scientist Paul Sniderman has challenged the conclusion that covert methods reveal more racism amongst whites, especially conservative American whites. Different versions of a survey were administered to different participants, where they were asked to respond to schemes for government assistance to laid-off workers some of whom were black or white, with work histories that showed some to be dependable and others to be unreliable, married or single, and with or without children. The research showed, surprisingly, that *conservative* white Americans were *more* likely to support government help to *black* workers than the whites in similar circumstances.

But what exactly can we conclude from these findings? A more detailed study of the findings shows that compared to liberals, conservative Americans were four times as likely to support state assistance to *dependable* black workers as compared with assistance to dependable white workers. But conservatives tended to regard black dependable workers as exceptions amongst black workers, and they supported government assistance to these workers as ones who, unlike other blacks, were 'really trying'.

That is, blacks were generally viewed by conservatives as not dependable, and in practice this means that only a small proportion of blacks were regarded as deserving of assistance. The rest were regarded as having only themselves to blame for their poorer fortunes, a view that would not support policies to reduce generalized black inequality in American society.

One plausible interpretation of such research findings is that while a large proportion of white Americans are now more prepared to support 'racial' equality, they are reluctant to support the specific policies that are required to address the unjust inequalities that have blighted the lives of African Americans, and this is partly because they regard such policies as possibly having a detrimental impact on their own economic interests and life chances. This would account for the inconsistencies and contradictions that seem to characterize the attitudes of white Americans to their black fellow citizens.

Human nature and the inevitability of racism

At this point it is useful to consider a view that has been briefly mentioned in my discussion of Enoch Powell and Le Pen. That is, underlying the view of many latter day racists and ultra-nationalists is the belief that what the critics decry as racism is simply the product of 'natural' human attributes such as the willingness of human groups, especially 'nations', to protect their 'own kind' and their own territories, forms of self-survival that inevitably involve acting defensively on the basis of stereotypes which may rest on limited knowledge but demonstrate sensible caution. What some see as a form of racism is thus viewed instead as thinking and behaviour that are and make 'common sense'. It is only 'human nature' to act in this manner. And, it is believed, this is just as well for the survival of individuals, cultures, and nations.

Evolutionary psychology, a recent development, is sometimes regarded as sanctioning racism as natural, but this is quite mistaken. The main researchers in the field, such as Cosmides and Tooby, are at pains to point out that their findings demonstrate the fundamental unity of the human species, thus completely undermining attempts to use their theories in support of interpretations that use the concept of race. And psychologists such as Steven Pinker, who do believe in some notion of human nature, are nevertheless quite clear that racism is not a universal feature produced by this human nature, although 'prejudice' and 'stereotyping' are inevitably involved in human attempts at classifying and responding to the social world.

A major problem with both the 'common sense' and more academic versions of biologically deterministic and evolutionary views of social behaviour is that on their own they are unable to account for *where* group boundaries are drawn, and *why*. There is nothing 'natural' about nations and nation-states, for example. They only emerged in modern times. To claim a basic biological continuity between defence of *national* territory, generalized xenophobia or hostility to 'foreigners' and a 'natural' preference for 'one's own kind' is misleading. 'One's own kind' may turn out to be a group based on gender, colour, religion, occupation, street, neighbourhood, village, city, country, or large agglomerate of nations such as contained within 'Europe' or the European Union.

There is a vacuity to the claim about racism being just 'human nature' that robs it of any historical or political specificity. Not all groups inspire loyalty or provoke hostility to the same degree in all periods. The extraordinarily diverse fate of Jewish communities in different cultures, times, and places furnishes a telling illustration of the implausibility of the 'human nature' thesis.

As an explanatory tool this version of the 'human nature' thesis is too vague to account for any particular defensiveness or hostility by any specific group towards another. Especially, it does not explain why and how groups have come to define themselves and others as 'races'. This is again a product of modern times, and closely connected to the idea of 'nations', from the 18th century onwards and has been the result of complex intellectual, political, cultural, and economic developments.

Stereotypes and scapegoats

Although 'stereotyping' and the exaggeration of similarities between members of one group and its differences as compared with another appear be more or less universal, this too does not explain why *particular* groups get labelled as having *specific* traits. What is clear from any historical analysis, for example of the British Empire and the noble savage, is that *contradictory* stereotypes or generalizations of 'Others' are usually in circulation at more or less the same time. The sexualization and gendering of race, as I have shown in earlier chapters, also plays an important role in complicating conceptions of racialized others.

The result is that *stereotypes*, like other views, reveal *contradiction* and *ambivalence* rather than completely invariable contempt or hostility or admiration towards other groups. The attributes of other groups tend to be split between 'good' and 'bad' ones. Attitudes towards Asians in Europe and the US, for instance, reveal admiration for supposed community unity, thrift, ambition, hard work, respect for education, and 'family values', but also hostility for insularity, suspicion regarding their loyalties to the Western nation-states in which they have come to live, and a sense of superiority towards their more 'backward' cultures, especially in relation to religion, the status of women, and so forth.

The supposed inevitability of racism is sometimes explained as the product of other kinds of innate psychological characteristics of humans. A common one is *scapegoating*.

Developing some ideas from Freud, the argument here is that when individuals or groups are unable to express their frustration and aggression against their real oppressors or exploiters because the latter are too powerful, the aggression becomes displaced onto weaker or lower-status individuals or groups unable to defend themselves. The targets are often ethnically distinct communities, especially if they are minorities, who are then attacked or discriminated against in some aggressive manner. At the individual level, the psychological mechanism involved is often referred to as *projection*, for which there is research evidence, whereby the individual displaces bad feelings about the self onto others as an unconscious defence and survival strategy.

Whatever the merits of such interpretations, the evidence is at best inconclusive. This is partly because of the inherent difficulties of studying unconscious mechanisms and motivations, and also because of the vague and speculative conceptions of instincts of aggression, death, and self-preservation that are posited.

One fundamental objection is that there is no conclusive research evidence that frustration and aggression are linked in the ways posited by the various scapegoating hypotheses. Frustration against the powerful may dissipate into fatalism, for example, or be undermined by perceived cultural and other commonalities with the powerful. And it is not clear that frustration is always present when aggression occurs. Aggression, moreover, as social learning researchers have demonstrated, is as much a learnt response as 'natural', and reliant for repetition upon social mechanisms and organizations which reward aggressive behaviour.

This immediately leads to the problem of how and why *particular* groups come to be the targets of the displacement of frustration-aggression, the role of political mobilization and ideological propaganda in this targeting, and why this might take a *racialized* form if it does at all. There is nothing *natural* or *inevitable* in one group – for example occupational rather than ethnic – being targeted rather than another, or biological elements such as skin colour acting as identifiers. Any fully fledged racism has to rely on the *prior* invention of the category of race and racialized interpretations of behaviour and cultural evaluation.

Whilst embodiment is obviously an important feature of human identities, and therefore what other human beings look like may create expectations about what they are like and how they might behave, the features that come to matter are historically learned and socially variable. There is nothing intrinsic in skin colour, shape of nose, or size of skull that has evoked similar responses. Indeed, dividing lines between skin colour, for example, are as much a matter of social processes as natural perception, as we have seen in the manner in which Italians and the Irish came to be 'seen' as 'white' in the USA, and in Britain too. And the failure of 'scientific racism' to provide consistent, credible classifications of nose or skull shape and other physiological features are equally telling.

Explanations of racism that rely on innate bio-psychological characteristics thus *presuppose* the existence of racism, and even then rely on questionable reasoning to establish connections between them.

Some psychoanalytic ideas are highly *suggestive* in interpreting the trans-historical persistence of ambivalence and sexualization in perceptions and interrelations between 'insiders' and 'outsiders'. Perhaps none is more compelling than Freud's insight regarding intrinsic, intertwining connections between love and hate, sexual desire and aggression, in relations between 'Self' and 'Other'.

Prejudice + Power = Racism?

In the period between the 1960s and 1980s, amongst a substantial proportion of white anti-racists in the USA and UK, it was common to define racism with the formula: 'Prejudice + Power = Racism'. But as I have shown in *'Race', Culture and Difference* (1992), only a modicum of analytical ability is required to have a field day with the oversimplifications involved.

The contradictions involved in the anti-racists' claim that prejudice is a product of *ignorance* and *irrationality* are easily exposed. Rectifying ignorance by factually undermining myths about blacks and other minorities can only work as an anti-racist strategy if the prejudiced are open to rational argument and evidence, which by definition the irrational are not.

Moreover, 'prejudice', in the form of expectations that go beyond immediate and interpersonal experiences and solidly verified truths about human behaviour appear to be universal human traits, not just confined to racists. This is clear from social psychological research on how individuals learn to classify and respond to the social world around them.

However, one should not entirely dismiss the fact that relative degrees of ignorance do nourish the formation of hostile attitudes. As many pointed out in response to Kilroy-Silk's statement that 'We Owe Arabs Nothing', it is in Arab cultures, indeed in present-day Iraq, that writing appears to have been invented, to take just one thing that 'we' owe 'Arabs'.

And what is one to make of hostility against minorities amongst relatively powerless white working class and poor whites? Could the poor never be classified as racist? This latter issue was pertinent given the view of many anti-racists that only whites could genuinely be regarded as racist, because only their prejudice could be translated into power against minorities. Of course, the formula also simply failed to accommodate the many relatively wealthy and powerful non-white individuals who expressed racist views.

Finally, the formula finds itself undermined by the argument that although most (white and other) individuals *might* have *unfavourable* or *unfriendly* views of '*outsiders*' or *strangers*, this does not constitute *racism*, which involves specific beliefs about the existence of races and the possibility of their being classified hierarchically as superior and inferior on a number of physiological and cultural criteria, amongst other things.

Chapter 8

Beyond institutional racism: 'race', class, and gender in the USA and Britain

Origins

The idea of 'institutional racism' goes back to the late 1960s in the USA, when Stokely Carmichael and Charles Hamilton used it in *Black Power* (1967), their powerful indictment of persistent black inequalities. Stokely and Carmichael wanted to highlight the process whereby, no matter whether the individual attitudes, motivations, and behaviour of ordinary white people were racist or not, all whites benefited from social structures and organizational patterns which continually disadvantaged blacks while allowing whites to stay well ahead in living standards, including housing, health and life span, neighbourhood amenities and safety, educational facilities and achievement, level of employment, and income and wealth.

They made it clear that this process could never be completely impersonal and unintentional. 'Institutional racism,' they argued, 'relies on the active and pervasive operation of anti-black attitudes and practices. A sense of superior group position prevails: whites are "better" than blacks . . . This is a racist attitude and it permeates the society, on both the individual and institutional level, covertly and overtly.'

'Institutional racism' was used to highlight the fact that the playing field in which blacks and whites competed for decent standards of living was not level. It was *systematically* skewed against blacks, both in terms of opportunities and outcomes. A vicious circle gripped black lives. A version of this view was officially accepted in the 1968 Kerner Commission's Report into ghetto uprisings. The Report argued that the USA was rapidly moving towards two societies, one black and one white, and it pointed to 'white racism' as the major underlying racial problem in American society.

In many respects, it seems, little has changed since. Studies such as Andrew Hacker's *Two Nations: Black and White, Separate, Hostile, Unequal* (1992), Douglas Massey and Nancy Denton's *American Apartheid: Segregation and the Making of the Underclass* (1993), and *Whitewashing Race: The Myth of a Colour-Blind Society* (2003) by Brown and his colleagues, amongst others, show how institutional racism continues to blight black lives. Inadequate housing, the product of years of discrimination and 'white flight', and poorly resourced schools lead to low educational achievement, lower admissions to colleges, and poor employment prospects. All of these are exacerbated by persistent hostility from white employers. The result is a cycle of high unemployment, drug taking, crime and unsafe neighbourhoods. Biased policing and courts and poor legal resources mean proportionately more arrests, convictions, and longer sentences. Black children thus grow up in an environment that systematically undermines their aspirations and leads to massive underachievement. The result is that black communities remain at the bottom of the American pile generation after generation.

Confusions

I will examine some of these processes in more depth later in this chapter. It is first necessary to chart the confusions that have bedevilled the idea of institutional racism, blunting and undermining its potential.

The concept has found more fertile soil in the UK than the USA. It acquired particular prominence when used in the officially commissioned report issued by Lord Scarman after his investigations into the black youth uprising in Brixton in South London in the early 1980s. But Scarman muddied the waters by restricting the idea to *intentional* racism – 'a society which knowingly, as a matter of policy, discriminates against black people' – and claiming that in this sense institutional racism did not exist in Britain. 'But', he went on to say, confusingly, 'racial disadvantage and its nasty associate racial discrimination have not been eliminated'.

Nearly 20 years later, Lord Macpherson's inquiry into the murder and police investigation of black teenager Stephen Lawrence in South London again focused public attention on institutional racism by claiming that, in part at least, it was to blame for the failure of the police operation to find the murderers. In his report of 1999, institutional racism was defined as:

> the collective failure of an organization to provide an appropriate and professional service to people because of their colour, culture or ethnic origin. It can be seen or detected in processes, attitudes and behaviour which amount to discrimination through unwitting prejudice, ignorance, thoughtlessness, and racist stereotyping which disadvantage minority ethnic people.

Already, we can see an unsystematic jumble of defining elements: *impersonal* processes, *conscious* attitudes and behaviour, and unwitting or *unintentional* prejudice.

In discussing the *origins* of unwitting racism, the report is equally muddled:

> lack of understanding, ignorance or mistaken beliefs. It can arise from well intentioned but patronizing words or actions. It can arise from unfamiliarity with the behaviour or cultural traditions

of people or families from minority ethnic communities. It can arise from racist stereotyping of black people as potential criminals or troublemakers. Often this . . . is born out of an inflexible police ethos . . . such attitudes can thrive in a tightly knit community . . . The police canteen can too easily be its breeding ground.

Further difficulties arise from the Macpherson Report's claim that it is not the 'policies of the police that are racist: it is rather the implementation of policies and . . . in the words and actions of officers acting together'.

Even leaving aside the subsequent extremely unhelpful suggestion in the report that a racist incident is one that is perceived as such by the victim, we are left floundering in a morass of confusions.

The report is not alone in this respect. Other official reports, national and municipal policy documents, social scientific research monographs, and anti-discriminatory legislation have left us with an equally confusing legacy, combining various forms of intentional and unintentional discrimination, including acts motivated by benign intentions and 'colour-blindness'.

There is also a tendency in descriptions of institutional racism to focus too exclusively on racism to the exclusion of other factors such as gender and class, especially. For example, police canteen culture is not merely a breeding ground for racism, it is also an arena in which policemen have to exhibit their masculinity and develop male bonding, which often involves using racist vocabulary and supporting racist views. Also, encounters between police and young black and Asian men are also contests of masculinity. Racialization and gender relations are intimately interwoven, and both need to be transformed for such encounters to take a less confrontational form.

The inquiry into the murder of an Asian schoolboy by a white boy at Burnage High School in Manchester in 1986 has been one of the few to recognize such complexity. The authors of the resulting report pointed out that the killing of Ahmed Iqbal Ullah was as much an outcome of the generalized culture of masculinized violence in the school as of racism and that the failure of the school's anti-racist policies owed much to the high-handed exclusion of white working-class parents by teachers from involvement in the formulation and workings of the school's anti-racist programme.

Moreover, it has become obvious that despite the emphasis by Macpherson and others on issues of unwitting prejudice, and thus the need for subtle but searching programmes of anti-racist education, there is a tendency for charges of institutional racism to result more in bureaucratic initiatives for ethnic monitoring (racial profiling as it is called in the US) and greater ethnic minority recruitment. Post-MacPherson, the London Metropolitan Police was embarrassed to find that the chief officer in charge of police anti-racism training had to resign following damaging evidence of racism.

Finally, it is striking that studies and reports on institutional racism unwittingly subvert the spirit of the original intention by focusing on single institutions such as the police or housing policies, while neglecting the systematic interconnections between discrimination in institutions such as housing, education, policing, and employment which create processes of cumulative disadvantage.

Beyond 'institutional racism': a radical proposal

Whatever the merits of the concept of institutional racism in the past in highlighting how chronic, systematic racism resulted not just from direct, intentional acts but also from practices and organizational cultures that led to indirect and unwitting discrimination, its use now confuses more than it clarifies and ends up doing more harm than good.

Arguably, the MacPherson Report, for instance, could have avoided unproductive controversy and a damaging backlash if instead of using the emotive and confusing charge of institutional racism it had confined itself to clearly identifying the ways in which various types of racism contributed to the failure of the police investigation, without implying or seeming to imply that they all formed a tightly interconnected web. The Report did not blame institutional racism for all the weaknesses of the police effort, but any caveats and complexities in the Report's comments on racism were drowned out in the controversy and backlash which followed.

The confusions endemic in the Report's usage of 'institutional racism' enabled many in the London Metropolitan Police to argue that no individuals could be held responsible for the failure of the investigation, which was instead attributed to organizational procedures, a collective ethos and unintentional prejudices. Others found a different defence from within the Report's confusions. That is, the argument was made that as an institution the police force simply reflected the society of which it was a part. Just as society had some racists, so the police barrel contained a few 'rotten apples'. Throw these out and the police force could be racism-free. This strategy, if allowed to proceed, would mean minimal reform and change in the collective culture, procedures, and accountability of the police.

Not everyone in the police force opposed reform, and many changes have since been introduced. But this supports the view that it is time for the notion of institutional racism to be discarded. All available research, documentation and experience suggests that different parts and individuals in organizations such as schools, business enterprises, the civil service, and the police force vary, often considerably, in the strength of their racism and level of commitment to equal opportunities policies. The internal structures, cultures and officers of institutions, if for the sake of convenience they are regarded as synonymous with organizations, do not constitute a seamless web. Very rarely do they consist of tightly interconnected sections and individuals with an identical ethos and pattern of operation.

Blanket accusations of 'institutional racism', against the mass media, for example, by Sir Ian Blair, London Metropolitan Police Commissioner, in January 2006 in connection with media coverage of murders of white and black young people, simply end up, as his did, in an unproductive debate in which the majority inside and outside the mass media felt convinced that the accusation unfairly homogenized a diverse sector.

There are numerous studies of the mass media which document in detail the selectivity of images and narratives involving ethnic minorities as well as the shortage of ethnic minority journalists and media producers. There is evidence, too, of attempts to remedy these biases and imbalances, although with limited effect. But a simple take-it-or-leave-it label of institutional racism only ended up strengthening lobbies that have campaigned against what they see as excessive 'political correctness'.

In the light of the confusions, lack of constructive debate and the formulation of clear policies that have flowed from the use of 'institutional racism', it seems clear that future discussions and policy proposals about racism should disaggregate the various direct and indirect, intentional and unwitting, operational and cultural sources and manifestations of racism and avoid a misleading bundling together of them within this muddled notion.

In social research, again, the idea of racialization, as proposed in an earlier chapter, highlighting varying degrees and types of racism is more useful than the concept of institutional racism.

And as we shall now see, the idea of institutional racism also has the disadvantage of focusing on only this one form of discrimination, when in fact many of the attitudes and procedures that discriminate against racialized populations also often disadvantage all poorer socio-economic groups or work against women from white and minority backgrounds. Many institutional practices and cultures combine masculinity, class, and racism in complex combinations, as the experience of women and homosexuals in the police, armed forces, and corporations reveal only too clearly.

However, it is important to retain the insights provided by various elements highlighted by the use of 'institutional racism'. Much of the racism that is perpetrated by those in positions of power and privilege, and experienced by those in subordinate positions in white majority societies such as the US and the UK now tends to be of a chronic, pervasive kind that does not necessarily make the news as major 'racist incidents'. Much hostility and discrimination against blacks, Hispanics, and Asians is not explicitly stated, especially to journalists or social researchers. Overt or visible behaviour, too, is likely to be polite, and hostility and discrimination are likely to be discussed and practised in less visible surroundings. Language may well be coded so that opposition is voiced against 'multiculturalism' rather than directly against non-whites. Segregation is often informal. Whites in the USA, Britain, and elsewhere often frequent restaurants, bars, and parks and take holidays where they are less likely to encounter blacks, Asians, and other ethnic minorities.

Also, the idea of institutional racism highlighted three other features of relevant social and economic processes that we must retain in any analysis of ethnic inequalities. Firstly, many such inequalities stem from an insistence on qualifications that may not be relevant. For example, in hiring practices in the US, an insistence on possession of high school diplomas and satisfactory performance on standardized tests excluded many blacks, especially for potential entry into skilled jobs and training despite the fact that it could not be demonstrated that the certificates and tests provided convincing evidence for ability to do particular jobs. Secondly, rules like school uniforms may not have been invented for purposes of discriminating against the dress codes of ethnic minorities who were not present when the rules were devised. Thirdly, inequalities are more often than not cumulative, so that poor housing, inadequate educational resources, and few local employment opportunities create cycles of disadvantage that are hard to break out of. Fourthly, processes such as the decline of old manufacturing industries in cities which developed on the basis of industries such as motor car manufacture, engineering, and textiles can hit ethnic minority and relatively recent immigrants harder partly because these are the urban areas and industries where they found employment during times when white workers found better work in other sectors and moved out of the inner city into suburbs. This is a systemic process that may not be related to racist intention, but has what one might see as racialized effects, with past patterns of discrimination also partly responsible for the consequence that racialized minority populations often bear the brunt of the loss of employment and the deterioration of other local facilities.

Systematic and durable inequalities

The idea of institutionalized racism may portray an exaggeratedly seamless web of racism, but we are nevertheless confronted with persistent patterns of stark, racialized inequalities in both the USA and Britain, despite decades of legislative and policy reform and a variety of initiatives to change disparaging views of ethnic minorities. And we are faced with the question of how such inequalities are to be explained, and especially to what degree racist discrimination accounts for such inequalities.

Gross inequalities persist in an era where legalized segregation has been abolished in the USA and where a series of legal and other reforms have diminished overt racism in the UK. Racialized inequalities are also a feature of the other major Western European nation-states such as France, Germany, and Italy.

Even a brief, broad overview of some of these inequalities makes for salutary reading. In the USA, in 2001, the real median income of black families was only 62% of that of whites, a figure that drops to 58% if Hispanics are excluded. And this is only 10% higher as a proportion than it was in 1947.

Unemployment rates for black men have remained stubbornly at at least twice that of all white men for a very long period, including the decades since the middle of the 20th century.

Black American children are almost three times as likely as white children to grow up in officially defined poverty. Not only are black children considerably more likely to be poorer, some two-thirds are more likely to grow up in low-income neighbourhoods than whites. This is because they are much more likely to grow up in segregated neighbourhoods.

African Americans remain the most residentially segregated group in the USA, partly because white Americans refuse to live in areas with more than 20% blacks. In addition, they are less likely to own a home, and when they do, they get less advantageous mortgage terms than whites. In general, blacks pay higher interest rates for mortgages for properties that are worth less than those of whites.

The differences in infant mortality rates, a stark indicator of the health of populations, are significantly large. Black infant mortality rates are twice those of whites, and this despite the fact that Medicaid support helped to drop black infant mortality rates by half between 1960 and 1980.

As Brown and his co-authors point out in *Whitewashing Race* (2003), where many of these findings are discussed, one key reason for these differences in health is the relative lack of access to primary medical care. In South Central Los Angeles, with a majority black and Latino population, the ratio of primary care doctors to the population is 1 to 12,993, compared to wealthier Bel Air where the ratio is 1 to 214.

Some 75% of African Americans now achieve a high school diploma. But only 14% earn a college degree. Given the differences in educational achievement, it is not surprising that while nearly half of all white men are in 'white collar' jobs, the proportion for blacks is less than one-third.

Striking disparities between American whites and blacks are to be found in crime and the criminal justice system. While blacks make up around 12% of the total population, they constitute 50% of the prison population, a figure that has risen from 29% in 1950.

Explaining black–white disparities in the USA: the role of racism

In many respects the situation of African Americans has improved in the second half of the 20th century, as is evident, for example, from the facts presented in Hacker's *Two Nations* (1992). In 1940, only 12% of blacks completed high school, compared with 82% in 1989. The black share of aggregate income has risen from 4.7% in 1947 to 7.2% in 1989.

Nevertheless, given the dramatic inequalities that still persist between blacks and whites, a careful but searching analysis is required to establish the extent to which blacks suffer because they continue to experience a variety of forms of racism in the criminal justice system, employment, housing, and education. The claim that black disadvantage continues to be the product of systematic past and present racism has been widely disputed, for example in scholarly publications by Abigail and Stephan Thernstrom, who argue that much of the inequality can be accounted for by unfavourable characteristics within black culture, and of course by those such as Herrnstein and Murray who believe that blacks have genetically derived inferior IQs compared to whites and Asians.

Let us look at the kind of disparity that suggests that racism affects what happens to blacks in the criminal justice system. Black defendants are more likely to be executed than white defendants. And those who commit crimes against black victims are less harshly punished than those whose victims are white.

A study by the US Department of Justice shows that between 1975 and 2000, 72% of death penalty prosecution approvals by the attorney-general were black, although there were an equal number of black and white perpetrators of murder. Race appears to be an important determining factor here. The vast majority of chief prosecutors are white, and chief prosecutors are more likely to enter plea bargaining agreements for whites than blacks. Moreover, the same study reveals, US attorneys were nearly twice as likely to seek the death penalty for black defendants accused of killing non-black victims than for black defendants accused of killing blacks.

Some part of the explanation lies in social class, as all poorer Americans are denied access to well-trained and properly funded lawyers. But there is little doubt that race plays a significant role in explaining the differential rates of capital punishment for blacks.

There is little doubt too about the systematic, severe inter-generational disadvantage suffered by African Americans, despite some of the benefits of affirmative action programmes.

The historical and continuing impact of racism on African American lives is hard to exaggerate. As some have remarked, for several centuries after the forced arrival of blacks from Africa as slaves from the 17th century onwards, they had to suffer under a system of *affirmative action for whites*. The formal emancipation of the slaves resulted only in an extraordinarily lop-sided playing field on which it was impossible for the blacks to enjoy equal opportunities without serious redress and redistribution to counter generations of cumulative inequality. The latter never occurred.

African Americans freed from slavery found the post-emancipation US a hostile and dangerous country with entrenched inequalities and high levels of official and unofficial opposition to black advancement. To take one telling example, from the 1860s to the 1930s, under the Federal Homestead Act the American government allocated at low or no cost some 246 million acres of land for farm homesteads, much of it taken from Native Americans, to about 1.5 million people, almost entirely from the white population. Meanwhile, legal segregation as well as mob violence and lynching in the Southern states ensured that formally free blacks were excluded from access to land, mineral and oil rights, and a large number of other government-controlled resources. Many blacks found themselves having to labour in the same plantations and fields as before, and their segregated schools, housing, and other facilities had a level of resources well below those enjoyed by the white population.

The descendants of slaves have found themselves caught in a series of cycles of poverty and institutionalized disadvantage. A United Nations survey of living standards in the 1990s ranked the quality of life of white Americans as the best in the world, while black Americans were placed 31st in the list.

I have already mentioned the continuing discrimination that blacks face in obtaining accommodation and the fact that they are more likely than any other American group to be in segregated areas with poor facilities of all kinds.

It is important to grasp that blacks also face continuing discrimination in employment right into the present, in addition to the fact that they are living in areas with poor employment opportunities. In 1996, for example, Texaco settled a case for $176 million with its African American employees for systematically denying them promotion. Social audit studies, which test for discrimination by sending white and non-white applicants with identical qualifications, consistently find that employers are less likely to offer interviews or jobs to non-whites.

Researchers have found that information about vacancies for a large number of jobs, in any case, are passed on by word of mouth to relatives, friends, and others in local networks, a process which has severely hampered the ability of blacks to break into job markets for a wide range of jobs in innumerable urban and rural areas. The impact of this type of networking, or what the sociologist Charles Tilly calls 'opportunity hoarding', has often been severe on black chances of employment, given the degree of segregation between black and white residence.

However, one type of explanation for black poverty and general disadvantage argues that blacks have been the victims of impersonal forces such as de-industrialization of old industries in the inner cities, as well as self-inflicted wounds such as demanding high wages, failing to enhance their skills, turning decent public housing and neighbourhoods into crime- and drug-ridden ghettos and no-go areas for white and other employers, aided by feckless women only too happy to have single-parent families and live off welfare.

Such accounts contain half-truths and exaggerations. In particular, they completely underestimate the extent to which blacks have found themselves facing blatant racial discrimination.

The wide gap between black and white rates of poverty pre-date the period of economic instability that started in the 1950s, and before the rise in the number of female-headed black families and any growth in welfare or transfer programmes. The first period of industrial restructuring and automation which impacted disproportionately on black workers in chemicals, steel, meatpacking, tobacco, and coal in cities such as Detroit and others in the South did so because blacks found themselves discriminated against by deliberately rigged restrictions and seniority rules which segregated them into jobs earmarked for automation. In addition, the new investment was concentrated in white areas even in states with large black populations.

The creation of black ghettos was aided by white flight – funded by federal approved loans – and the 'positive racial policy' of concentrating black families in public housing which inevitably concentrated and contained black poverty in specific areas of the inner city. It is hardly surprising that by the mid-1990s the median net worth of white households was worth *ten* times that of black (and Latino) households.

All of this has been overlain on a deeply entrenched system of inequalities in educational facilities, especially in the South as a result of decades of legalized segregation before the Civil Rights legislation of the 1960s. It is not surprising that in the wake of desegregation and a real Federal push against poverty throughout the country, blacks made substantial educational gains in the 1970s and 1980s as measured by test scores in reading and maths.

Affirmative action and the new black middle class

Conservative criticism and general controversy has loomed particularly large over affirmative action policies for blacks in education. Moreover, the eminent black sociologist William Julius Wilson has been arguing since 1978, when he published *The Declining Significance of Race*, that in the post-affirmative action period since the 1970s black life chances are now increasingly more dependent on their social class background than their 'race'.

The success of affirmative action policies for blacks is at the heart of these debates. The initiative first came in an executive order from President Kennedy in 1963. Its aims were to end direct and unintentional discrimination by individuals and institutions, and to redress the huge historical imbalance by providing for quotas to assist blacks. The 1964 Civil Rights Act thus included a ban on racial discrimination by employers.

However, the historical record suggests that charges of indirect discrimination against employers are rarely brought to court, and even cases of direct discrimination are difficult to win because of the difficulty of establishing unambiguous intent to discriminate. Moreover, a series of Supreme Court decisions have whittled away the power of institutions to operate quotas.

Nevertheless, it is undeniable that in the post-1960s period the African American population has made significant gains. And it cannot be doubted that the increase in black representation in the legal profession, medicine, education and business corporations owes much to the existence of affirmative action legislation.

The African American new middle class, however, pays a 'race' penalty in lower earnings than middle-class whites, less preferential mortgages for house purchase, and residential segregation in largely black suburbs near city limits where lower property prices perpetuate a gap in wealth and assets in comparison with equivalent whites. It may be less apparent, but the black middle class remains as segregated from whites as poor blacks.

These facts have forced Wilson to revise his earlier analysis. In his 1999 *The Bridge Over the Racial Divide*, he now argues that some form of 'race'-specificity is required to ensure that African Americans are protected against discrimination.

Under the pressures of industrial and commercial collapse, housing decay, and the decline in public services, inner city areas, especially those with majority black locales are imploding. Crime and drug-related offences are at an all-time high. Homicides between black men have been escalating to the point where this is the most likely cause of death for young black males. Nearly 30% of black men will spend some time in a federal or state prison.

The enduring power of 'race' and racism

In a speech in 1965 endorsing the end of legal discrimination, President Lyndon B. Johnson pointed out that this could not by itself usher in a new historical era of equal opportunities for African Americans. As he put it, 'You do not take a person who for years has been hobbled by chains, and liberate him, bring him up to the starting line, and then say, "You are free to compete with all the others."'

How right he was. Half-hearted affirmative action, amongst other things, has led to some limited gains by America's black population. But African Americans continue to experience severe disadvantage.

However, even poor whites seem unsympathetic to the plight of their black neighbours. Surveys amongst poor whites reveal strong hostility to blacks receiving the same state aid that has benefited these whites. The reason is the same as that given by middle-class whites. A majority of white Americans appear to believe that more often than not blacks have only themselves to blame, for they are lazy, or lack sufficient intelligence, and refuse to make the best of the chances they have generously been offered.

This is indeed a form of racism, which continues alongside other versions. Some have called it a '*laissez-faire* racism' because it now leaves the fate of the blacks to inherently imbalanced markets. Its rallying cry is colour-blindness as a non-racist principle, although its views of poorer African Americans appear to be (often ambivalently) disparaging.

Deep divisions between whites and blacks erupt and become only too visible at certain points. The beating of the black motorist Rodney King in Los Angeles and the subsequent not guilty verdict by a white jury in 1992 against the policemen responsible for the brutal attack, filmed only by chance, led to widespread protests and disturbances by the black population of Los Angeles and other cities. The trial of the black former footballer O. J. Simpson, accused of murdering his white wife and her white friend, completely divided America along a black–white fault line, with a majority of whites believing him to be guilty, while the bulk of

African Americans remained sceptical of the charges brought against him.

Predictably, nothing changed in the wake of O. J. Simpson's acquittal on 3 October 1995. And recent research makes it clear how separate are the frames through which whites and blacks view American society. Whites believe that serious racial discrimination is a thing of the past, while blacks endure daily racial slights and have no doubt that they have to struggle against deeply embedded structures and attitudes which disadvantage them from the start.

A rigorous analysis of the cultural divisions and patterns of inequality in the USA supports no other conclusion than that racism survives, indeed can even thrive, in the most affluent and one of the most liberal democracies of the modern world. Generations of blacks, and now Latinos, will continue to find their life chances hampered by forms of racism from the most direct to ones that operate impersonally, structurally, and cumulatively.

Post-imperial panics: ethnic segregation and 'race riots' in 21st-century Britain

British Race Relations legislation has often been held up as a model for the rest of the European Union. Yet, nearly 30 years after the seminal 1976 Act, which added indirect discrimination as a punishable offence, Trevor Phillips, Chair of the Commission for Racial Equality, was warning the country that it was in danger of 'sleepwalking' into 'segregation'. How had Britain, with its self-image of a liberal, tolerant, and fair-minded nation, and its official adoption of multiculturalism, come to be on the verge of what was described by many as 'a US-type nightmare'?

The official inquiries into the 'mill town' disorders of the northern British cities did indeed paint a picture of white and Asian communities increasingly separated in patterns of residence, schooling, friendship, and employment.

Moreover, the reports into the disorders in the northern cities pointed out that the areas involved were amongst the poorest 20% in the country, and some of the more specific urban wards where the South Asian and white populations involved lived were actually in the poorest 1% of the whole country.

Why were many British Asians, mostly of Pakistani and Bangladeshi origin and Muslim in faith, and the African Caribbeans, now well on the way to falling into a condition resembling that of American blacks?

Keeping out the 'undesirables': the untold story of British immigration policy towards black and Asian immigration to post-1945 Britain

In 1998, Britain celebrated the 50th anniversary of the arrival to Britain of 492 Jamaicans aboard the *SS Empire Windrush*, marking the beginning of the postwar immigration of black and Asian colonial and postcolonial subjects to what many of them fondly thought of as the 'mother' country. Some had already been in Britain, serving in the armed forces.

The official story of this immigration suggests that Britain opened its arms and welcomed the black and Asian migrants, especially given the desperate need for labour as the British economy began its postwar reconstruction and the welfare state, especially the National Health Service, was established and expanded. Most of the blacks and Asians who came had the right of free entry given to them by the British Nationality Act of 1948 which made colonials into British subjects of the Crown.

And, so the accepted narrative goes, British governments only reluctantly introduced a series of restrictions to 'coloured' immigration, beginning with the 1962 Act, in order to preserve 'good race relations' by appeasing those white British who objected to the arrival and settlement of black and Asian neighbours and workmates.

But, as official records have now revealed, the British Labour Government of Attlee was horrified when it learnt that the *Empire Windrush* was to set sail. The British policy was to recruit white workers, especially Eastern Europeans displaced during the war. Attlee immediately dubbed those aboard the *SS Windrush* 'undesirable elements', and frantic but unsuccessful attempts were made immediately to prevent the ship from sailing.

To prevent any more *Windrush*s from setting sail, Colonial Office functionaries were dispatched to lobby administrations in the West Indies and India, and every attempt was made to convince would-be migrants that the availability of jobs in Britain was a myth. The British Government's lie was soon exposed. A desperate London Transport, and the Ministry of Health, subsequently to be headed by Enoch Powell, who enthusiastically recruited West Indian nurses, initiated recruitment drives in the Indian subcontinent and the West Indies.

Government papers now declassified reveal that official discussions in the Home Office and other departments were driven by strongly held colonial stereotypes of blacks and South Asians. They were regarded, variously, as lazy, quarrelsome, and prone to criminality. The racism that permeated these discussions was thoroughly sexualized. Fears were expressed in Ministerial committees about the degenerative consequences of miscegenation. Sexual liaisons between black men and white women were a continuing nightmare for the officials. White working-class women, especially, were regarded as too attracted to black men.

And as I have argued in my essay on 'Racialization' and elsewhere, there has been a strong racist element to immigration and nationality policies throughout the post-1945 period. The 1948 Nationality Act, for example, allowed freedom of entry from the colonies and ex-colonies only on the assumption that almost all of those who would come to the UK would be *whites* from the 'old Commonwealth' of Australia, New Zealand, and Canada.

Racial discrimination and ethnic inequalities in Britain

The patterns of immigration and discrimination that characterized the postwar period led, not surprisingly, to a distinct and disadvantaged place for Britain's growing 'coloured' minority.

Overt discrimination has continued despite anti-discrimination legislation. Just as in the American case, its operations have dipped further under the surface and have had to be revealed by 'social audit' techniques.

A well known study by Brown and Gay in 1985 suggested that 'colour' discrimination in the period since 1968 had remained at similar levels. Using actors as well as matched applications for vacancies they found that at least a third of employers continued to discriminate against non-whites for jobs. More recent local studies have confirmed this pattern of discrimination. Analysis by the Oxford University sociologist Anthony Heath of Census information at a national level in the 1990s suggests, again, that black and Asians continue to suffer what has come to be called an 'ethnic penalty' that is the same as that experienced by the first generation.

In the light of these studies, the cases mentioned in the first chapter of Asian doctors having to be paid compensation for discrimination by the National Health Service should come as no surprise. In particular, they confirm that high qualifications and skills gained by ethnic minorities are no guarantee of immunity against discrimination by employers, but also that in the professions and managerial grades there appears to be a 'glass ceiling' which curtails promotion opportunities and prevents 'coloured' minorities from obtaining full rights to equal treatment.

However, there is also general agreement amongst researchers that some ethnic minority groups in particular have made improvements to their relative position since the 1980s. These are primarily people of Indian, African Asian (mostly Indians from East and Central Africa), and Chinese origin.

Analysis of the 2001 Census shows that Indians and African Asians now have between 17% and 20% of their population in professional occupations, compared to the 11% registered by the white British, but the continuing disparity in managerial and employer categories indicate the continuing existence of a glass ceiling, based in some variable part on discrimination. The African Caribbean population finds itself over-represented in manual occupations, but it is the figures for those of Bangladeshi origin which are the most striking, with two-thirds of them in lower-level manual employment.

African Caribbean women have made the most progress in job level among female employees, even outstripping white and African Asian women.

Unemployment rates have shown a stubborn consistency over a long period, with ethnic minorities being twice as likely to be unemployed. Also, members of the minorities are twice as likely to live in poverty as whites, and 60% of British Pakistani and Bangladeshi people live in poverty.

Amongst British ethnic minority groups, as within the American black population, growing divergence and even polarization is becoming evident, with people of Bangladeshi and Pakistani origin, and some part of the black population increasingly confined to the bottom of all the important socio-economic indicators of earnings, occupation and poverty.

To what extent are the patterns of inequality suffered by the ethnic minorities a product of easily identifiable racial discrimination? All ethnic minorities, as we have seen, continue to incur an 'ethnic penalty' in relation to identical qualifications and experience when their earnings and occupational levels are examined, and this is an indication of continued discrimination, confirmed by social audit studies. There has also been collusion between white workers and their trade unions, and employers, to ensure the restriction of promotion opportunities to white workers.

But other factors also need to be taken into account. Compared to the rural background and low level of education of immigrants of Bangladeshi origin, Indians and African Indians in particular were on average better educated, economically more successful, and have had greater familiarity with the English language. This has allowed them to make better use of educational opportunities and the Chinese population too has shown remarkable success levels.

Moreover, Pakistani migrants and their children are heavily concentrated in areas in the North and the Midlands that have suffered a severe decline in manufacturing, especially textiles and engineering. Bangladeshis are concentrated in areas where there is a combination of poor housing and schooling resources and fewer employment opportunities.

Housing is another sphere in which a large number of studies have revealed discrimination and disadvantage against ethnic minorities, although again this is only part of the story. Analyses have shown that in London, the Midlands, and the north, ethnic minorities are concentrated in the poorer residential areas. Also, ethnic minorities are less likely than whites to own their own homes. And when they do own houses, they are likely to occupy the oldest housing, in the worst state of repair. In public housing, a large number of local studies have revealed that, partly as a result of intentional discrimination, ethnic minorities receive a disproportionate share of the least popular housing in the least desirable estates.

Ethnic segregation in general is not near American levels, although it is undoubtedly the case that in some cities of the north, such as Bradford, Burnley, and Oldham, where young Asians, white youth and police clashed in 2001, white and non-white communities live largely 'parallel' lives, with separate residential areas and schools and very little inter-communal socializing.

As in employment and earnings, the British Bangladeshi and Pakistani populations are the most disadvantaged, occupying the worst housing in the least desirable areas. Investigations continue to show that over 20% in fact live in properties that according to the English House Conditions Survey are 'the worst in the country'.

Ethnicity, education, and achievement

Social audit studies and broad measures of 'ethnic penalties' are useful as indicators of racial discrimination, but fail to get at the texture of day-to-day racism, in all its variety, contradiction, and ambivalence. Only detailed ethnographic studies reveal the complexity of racism as expressed in encounters between the various ethnic groups that make up contemporary British society. Some of the best of these studies have been conducted in schools, as I have argued elsewhere, as researchers attempt to understand the processes that explain how and why the different experiences of white, Asian, and black girls and boys lead to differences in attitudes to education and a variety of patterns of achievement.

In particular, we need to turn to these studies to get some purchase on an issue that is now seen as crucial: the different roles of racism and a supposedly pathological black masculinity in explaining what appears to be catastrophic underachievement amongst black boys in British schools, a debate that carries more than an echo of panics over black males in American culture. At the same time, this allows us to probe further into a theme I have consistently highlighted in this book and in other publications: the complex interplay between racism, class, gender, and sexuality.

As revealed in the British Census of 2001, the lowest levels of high school achievement as measured by GCSE attainment were amongst pupils of Afro-Caribbean origin, with 23% of boys and 38% of girls achieving grades A*–C. Chinese and Indians had the highest success rates: 77% of Chinese girls and 71% of Chinese boys, and 70% of Indian girls and 58% of Indian boys achieving five or more GCSE grades A* to C. Within each ethnic group, a higher proportion of girls than boys achieved these levels.

The permanent exclusion rate for black Caribbean pupils, at 42 per 1,000, was three times the rate for white pupils.

Not surprisingly, given the schooling achievements, among men the black Caribbeans were the least likely to have degrees, at 8%, while at present nearly half of all young people of Chinese and Indian origin enter higher education, 50% higher than the rate for whites.

There is an important social class effect. Amongst the entire population, including African Caribbean men and women, the largest proportions or university entrants are from non-manual backgrounds. The most striking achievements against the grain of social class disadvantage come from the Indian, Pakistani, Chinese, and Bangladeshi households, where more than one-third of all their entrants come from manual backgrounds compared to just a quarter for whites and black Caribbeans.

How does racism appear to affect these patterns? Ethnographic studies of school life reveal quite a high level of teacher hostility to boys of African Caribbean origin and many Asian pupils as well. Studies show that the same behaviour is likely to be interpreted more unfavourably if African Caribbean boys are involved, whether this is inattention and insubordination in class, or infraction against school rules such as hairstyles that have been forbidden. This is one reason why African Caribbean boys have a higher rate of exclusion from schools. African Caribbean boys of similar ability to other pupils are also likely to find themselves in lower sets and streams.

Lower teacher expectations, negative stereotypes and racist slurs have now been too often revealed as a cause of depressed performance by African Caribbean boys to be ignored, as I have shown in *'Race', Culture and Difference* (1992). Teacher racism is often compounded by black boys' harassment by police outside schools, and the unwillingness of schools to understand or tackle such unfair and alienating treatment. Moreover, black boys are seen as physically threatening, especially by women teachers, and there appears to be more than an undercurrent of the continued circulation of the notion of the black male as sexual predator which affects how the black boys are viewed.

However, it is also clear that this is not a simple case of unremitting racism by white teachers against blameless black male students. Firstly, it is also clear from the detailed studies that *black* male and female teachers are often equally hostile to black boys. Secondly, there are a great many white teachers who do not engage in negative stereotyping, get on well with black boys, and are sympathetic to the black boys' complaints of racism inside and outside the school. Thirdly, confrontations between teachers and pupils are often as much about masculinity and resistance to supposed threats to 'manliness' on the part of black boys as about race *per se*. Fourthly, the responses of black boys vary enormously. Even amongst those who feel unfairly treated many refuse to get into confrontations with teachers and try their best to get on with schoolwork. In this respect, they follow a strategy more common amongst black girls who may show some disaffection, but keep it low enough to avoid exclusion and meanwhile work hard to obtain qualifications.

However, the black boys who do attempt to succeed and follow the behavioural codes laid down by the school have to face taunts of 'acting white', being 'batty' (gay), or 'pussies' (girls). And a variable proportion of black boys are into forms of 'street culture' which develop into hedonistic, violent, ganja smoking, and generally anti-school forms which make it difficult for more educationally committed boys to retain credibility and resist accusations that they are betraying their communities.

A minority of black boys are part of often violent gangs, as are Asians. As a major researcher into these issues, the black British sociologist Tony Sewell has pointed out many black boys deliberately play up to an aggressive, macho, highly sexualized image, using it as a resource in power struggles with teachers, police, parents, and pupils of white and Asian origin.

Educational underachievement is as much a cause for worry amongst white boys of working-class origin. And there is a more general occupational and income polarization amongst all ethnic groups which is a consequence of neo-liberal government policies.

Is Britain less racist now?

A good case can be mounted for the proposition that Britain is less racist now than, say, nearly four decades ago when Enoch Powell made his infamous 'Rivers of Blood' speech, predicting a racial blood-bath in Britain in the years to come. Recently Powell's local Conservative Party adopted a British Asian woman to stand in his Parliamentary seat (although she suffered the same fate as another of Powell's successors, being swept away in the wake of Labour's national successes).

While there have indeed been what have popularly been called 'race riots', even as recently as 2001, this type of disaffection amongst blacks, Asians, and whites has never reached the horrific levels projected by Powell's image of London's version of the Roman Tiber foaming with blood.

All the ethnic minorities have experienced educational and occupational improvement since the late 1960s. Their presence seems to be an accepted part of the British urban landscape. Governments have praised the economic contribution they have made, far outweighing whatever costs immigration brought. The minorities have acquired greater visibility and power in Parliament, business, the professions, and the media. Their cultural influence has also been much lauded. Chicken tikka massala has been proclaimed the national dish. Black and South Asian music and styles have spawned a wide range of cross-overs, hybrid forms, and imitators. Britain has the highest rate of intermarriage between whites and blacks of anywhere in Europe. Many young white, black, and Asian youth have now developed shared, hybrid linguistic styles in inner urban areas.

So, there is obviously some truth in the suggestion that Britain is less racist than it was, indeed, in some ways it has become an established and vibrant multicultural society in a form unimaginable in the depressing 1950s when there was widespread overt hostility to blacks in search of housing, employment, and a drink at the local pub.

But racism can thrive in a whole variety of guises under the surface. And it remains raw and bloody too. The racist murders of the black teenagers Stephen Lawrence and several Asians are stark reminders. Official investigations into prisons and the police reveal a disturbing amount of abuse and discrimination. Teacher racism is a not inconsiderable obstacle, as shown by a number of research studies. Social audit studies of hiring practices of private companies, and adding up the costs of compensation payments for racial discrimination by the National Health Service and other agencies also reveal how stubbornly racism can remain embedded in managerial cultures and practices. Voting for the openly racist British National Party has reached unprecedented levels in London's East End and in many northern towns.

Hysteria against refugees and asylum seekers is highly racialized, with blacks and Asians figuring large in the demonology. The threat of Islamic terrorism has fuelled hostility to Muslims, although as I have argued earlier, 'Islamophobia' is too crude a notion to capture the forms of anti-Muslim sentiment.

The reader should heed the message of this book that racism is multidimensional, with varying degrees of cultural, colour and other physiological coding. Nor is it is not an all or nothing phenomenon. It is marked by deep ambivalence and contradiction. Nothing illustrates this better than the variety of responses that exist around South Asian culture in Britain. Its cultural image varies between thrifty and flashy, admirable in its support for family values but oppressive to women, passive but also spawning dangerous gang cultures, 'modern' in its belief in education and commercial success, 'pre-modern' in its backward adherence to arranged and forced marriages and its attachment to religion, and yet, simultaneously, too 'post-modern' in its extensive global networks that allow it to transcend so easily the limits of the nation.

Moreover, as I have also argued, a range of attitudes and propensity to discriminate co-exist in the same white individuals and organizations. It is unclear how much of the acceptance accorded the non-white minorities is grudging, resigned, conditional, and accompanied by resentment that can turn into discrimination if opportunities arise and chances of detection are limited. The gradual movement of whites away from urban areas, and the discomfort of blacks and Asians in the British countryside, may only be the visible tip of a larger, seething, ambivalent hostility.

Conclusions: prospects for a post-racial future

In 1903, the black American sociologist Du Bois predicted that 'the problem of the twentieth century is the problem of the colour-line'. In 2006, the British historian Niall Ferguson published what has been billed as a major new interpretation of the 20th century. Seemingly unaware of Du Bois, Ferguson argues in *The War of the World* that the idea of 'race' and the way it became interwoven with ethnicity and the collapse of multinational empires was one of the main drivers, perhaps the key underlying factor, in the determining conflicts of the century.

Arguably, both Ferguson and Du Bois have been guilty of exaggeration. Yet there is much to commend Du Bois's foresight and Ferguson's historical overview. However, a case could as easily be mounted for the centrality of 'race' to the 19th century as well. If so, what are the prospects that such a crucial and deeply embedded idea will not be important in the 21st century? What are the prospects for a post-racial future?

Before embarking, albeit briefly, on a discussion of such a momentous question, we need to be clear about what the question means. This requires a return to a view I have expressed throughout. That is, conflicts between geo-cultural groups have of course been a perennial part of human history, and some or other combination of ethnic, linguistic, and religious boundaries has been crucial in creating prejudice and hostility. Each culturally and geographically bounded group has been prone to see the world and its other inhabitants through its own ethnocentric frame, although it is important to remember that these frames are themselves subject to internal fracturing along cross-cutting economic, cultural, gender, and smaller geo-political fault lines. Each group and subgroup has its stereotypes of others as 'barbarians'. But as the historical, anthropological, and psychological evidence also shows, there is no necessary translation of group loyalty into hostility to other groups.

However, the idea of race as it developed from the 18th century onwards, while bearing strong traces of earlier ethnocentricisms, created a novel frame for the classification and evaluation of human groups, based around new biological understandings and geo-cultural, especially *national*, conceptions of 'natural' human boundaries, divisions, and essences. Once the genie of race was out of the bottle, its effects and influence spread far beyond its European and then American areas of origin. Japanese, Chinese, and many Indian intellectuals and political elites were seduced and became obsessed with conceptions of racial purity, racial essences, and the expulsion of alien, contaminating elements embodied by groups with distinct, or supposedly distinct, geographical, linguistic, and religious origins.

After the invention of 'race', all geo-cultural and geo-political conflicts have had the potential to be racialized, a striking new element having the potential to provide scientific legitimation for wiping out entire 'alien' populations. In thinking about the potential for a post-racial future, we have to be aware that what we are contemplating are the chances that the distinctive and lethal combination of science, physiological classification, and cultural evaluation that came into being in the late 18th century will no longer exercise the power it has had in the 19th and 20th centuries. However difficult it is, now, and always has been, to distinguish ethnicity and ethnocentrism, prejudices and stereotyping, from race and racism more strictly conceptualized, nevertheless, the question we have to pose is about the possibility that conflicts between human groups and individuals can and will be significantly less *racialized* in the 21st century. It is important to bear in mind my earlier argument that discussions of these issues need to get away from simple dichotomies between 'racist' and 'non-racist'. The question that we have to address is not whether some or other idea of race will completely vanish from the culture and politics of the future and whether all discrimination based on notions of race will disappear. What has to be gauged is the degree to which 'race' will continue to figure, as part of the processes of racialization, in combination with associated ideas of cultural boundaries around ethnicity and the nation, and legal issues of citizenship.

Given the variety of forms that race and racism have taken, in combination with ethnicity, nationality, religion, and sexuality, and also given the significance of ambivalence and contradiction in individual and group identities, the question can only be answered in very broad and speculative terms.

Grounds for optimism

A hundred years ago, few in Europe and America doubted that the world's human population could be divided into separate races, each with its own distinctive physiology and cultural characteristics. And hardly anyone in Europe and America doubted that the white man had an inherited superiority which accounted for and legitimized the West's rule over so much of the globe.

In 2006, such views are substantially less common and certainly less openly held. At present the balance of scientific opinion is definitely weighted against the credibility of racial theories of the type taken for granted a hundred years ago. Belief in *The Bell Curve* doctrine of the genetic inferiority of blacks is limited and muted. Overt racisms of the kind institutionalized in segregation legislation in the Southern states in the USA and the Apartheid system of

South Africa have suffered mortal blows, although it is worth reminding ourselves that American segregationism was only seriously challenged in the 1960s and that the Apartheid regime fell apart just over a decade ago. The countries where racism, properly so-called, originated now have laws that aim to protect groups and individuals from direct and indirect racial discrimination.

But if it is difficult to quantify degrees of racism, the evidence is unambiguous that racism is still a problem as we start the 21st century. And there are several indicators that point to its continuing, and even growing, influence.

Colour, culture, and belonging: the continuing spectre of race

New findings in genetics are continuing apace, and many of these will continue to be pressed into service by diehard believers in the reality of race. One of the latest in what will no doubt be a flourishing literature is by the Americans Sarich and Miele, *Race: The Reality of Human Differences* (2005). Even a cursory look reveals weak arguments and disingenuousness akin to that of the authors of *The Bell Curve*. But more plausible reasoning is also present, and more rigorous and heavy-weight attempts will certainly follow. These are likely to get the same media attention as *The Bell Curve*, and their views will be circulated and recycled in a range of other popular publications and will be promoted by racist organizations.

The rise in support for neo-fascist and other overtly racist extreme right-wing movements in the last decade of the 20th century is one of the most obvious indicators that strong racism may have growing appeal in the very countries where the idea of race was invented and then apparently comprehensively defeated.

The most dramatic moment in the rise of the far right in Europe came in the French presidential elections of 2002. Le Pen, leader of the neo-fascist Front National, emerged as the runner-up, with 5.5 million votes. Elsewhere, the Vlaams Blok in Belgium, the Northern League and the more openly fascist MSI in Italy – the MSI in the form of the Alleanza Nazionale having entered the coalition government of Sylvio Berlusconi – the Freedom Party (FPO) in Austria, which entered government in 2000, and the support for Pym Fortuyn's anti-immigration campaign in Holland have all registered substantial successes that have seemed unimaginable given the stigma and revulsion against fascism, extreme nationalism, and racism in the post-Second World War period. The British National Party has gained numerous seats in local elections in northern cities and London's East End. In Switzerland, the Swiss People's Party (SVP) won the largest share of the vote in the 2003 general election. Russia and all the Eastern European countries now have growing extreme right parties which are ultra-nationalist, anti-Semitic, and opposed to liberal democracy.

The re-emergence of openly racist parties has complex causes. And the degree and form of their racism and its admixture with various types of nationalism and regionalism also vary between the different European countries.

All the extreme right parties profess a commitment to one or other version of the 'new racism' discussed earlier, with an emphasis on nation and culture. However, more biologically based versions of 'race' form perennial subtexts that emerge more openly at some times than others. Amongst the Swiss SVP's election posters, to take just a single instance, was one with a caricatured black face and the message 'The Swiss are increasingly becoming Negros'.

Indeed, the immediate catalyst for the success of the revived extreme right in Europe is the mobilization of insecurity and disaffection stemming from the supposed threats to the nation, its identity and prosperity, posed by 'coloured' immigrants from the poverty-stricken regions of Africa, Asia, and Latin America. Their numbers have increased with the addition of refugees and asylum seekers as postcolonial states in former Western empires have imploded.

The electoral success of the extreme right shows no real signs of falling off, although support for them is volatile. Part of the success of the extreme right lies in its ability to exploit more generalized disaffection with mainstream parties, economic insecurity deriving from the collapse of old industrial sectors, and the consequent growth in unemployment, and the weakening of older solidarities based on class. The latter process has obviously accelerated after the spectacular crisis of older socialist political movements.

However, this also means that support for the extreme right parties cannot be automatically interpreted as a support for racism *per se*. As previously in Nazi Germany, it is also part protest and generalized disaffection.

In both Europe and the USA, racialization is fed by a backlash against 'multiculturalism' in which the positions of the extreme and the mainstream right often overlap to a considerable extent, assisted by a common over-reaction over issues of refugees and asylum seekers.

In Britain, a crisis of multiculturalism has been officially proclaimed, especially in the wake of disorders involving Muslim South Asian youth in the northern cities and fears of Asian ghettos. A government-sponsored campaign has begun, to replace multiculturalism with a call for settled non-white minorities to integrate and assimilate to a greater degree. As many of us have pointed out, the panic over multiculturalism fails to notice the degree to which second and third generations of Asian and black youth actually embrace British identity. Moreover, 'integration' is poorly defined, as are the core British values to which all are supposed to subscribe. In the USA, the backlash against a more inclusive national culture has taken the form of campaigns against so-called 'political correctness', hostility to the remaining vestiges of affirmative action, and support for 'colour-blind' policies.

Slogans such as 'France for the French', 'Rights for Whites', and complaints that whites have become second-class citizens in their own countries have a wide resonance. Their appeal, suitably repackaged, is not confined to deprived areas and amongst disadvantaged white populations. Liberal, centre-left, and conservative middle classes and intellectuals have been making common cause in Europe around a generalized defence of national identity.

The increasing powers of supra-national entities such as the European Union, the forces of economic globalization which have involved the outsourcing of jobs to India and China, and the threat of a resurgent, militant global Islam are creating conditions in which broad cultural and political coalitions are being united by varying degrees of nationalism. And as Billig has demonstrated in an insightful discussion, forms of 'banal', everyday nationalism constantly reinforce limiting senses of national identity.

While forms of progressive nationalism are possible, it is important to remember the close intertwining of *nation* and *race*, both historically and in the present. Debates around the crisis of national identity in each of the nation-states of Europe have a variable racial element, with the defence of national and ethnic exclusiveness always liable to shade off into support for European nations as communities of *whites*. Softer versions of nationalism in European nation-states are still based on the underlying idea that the nation must remain a majority white population. Colour, that is, eventually trumps culture. After all, there is no suggestion within progressive nationalisms that even in principle it would be acceptable for the British, French, or German nations to be composed of a majority of perfectly assimilated blacks, for example. Sometimes, as in debates over the place of Turkey, Christian exclusivity may combine both religion and race.

Given that anxieties around national identity in the context of European unification, globalization, pressures for migration into the richer European and American North, and militant Islam will continue with the same intensity, and developments in genetics will always be open to racialized interpretation and re-interpretation, the prospects for a 21st century in which 'race' will have a steadily diminishing role to play seem small. But it would take quite exceptional scientific, cultural, and political transformations for there to be a return to the taken-for-granted assumption of the reality of race and the superiority of white populations that was so widespread and uncontested at the start of the 20th century.

On the other hand, conceptions of the present as dominated by a 'clash of civilizations', as popularized by the American political scientist Samuel Huntington, have often been given strong racial overtones and have easily intertwined with religious and other forms of cultural exclusivity, as evidenced by controversies over the admission of Turkey to the European Union, and by discussions of Muslim minorities in the European nation-states.

Moreover, one of the disturbing effects of conflicts such as those in the Middle East is the recycling of racialized stereotypes. On the one hand, crude anti-Semitism has been given a new lease of life in Egypt and Saudi Arabia and has been encouraged by the new Iranian President's Holocaust denials. On the other, witness the opinion expressed by the former Israeli leader Erhud Barak in an interview to the British newspaper the *Guardian* in May 2002, while reflecting on his Camp David negotiations. 'Arabs', he said, 'don't suffer from the problem of telling lies that exists in Judaeo-Christian culture', thus neatly combining race, geography, and culture in a formulation that captures the manner in which common-sense racialization seems set to continue.

National and ethnic conflicts throughout the globe continue to take racialized forms. The political and economic conflict in Rwanda between Hutus and Tutsis was often given racial connotations by the description of Tutsis as taller and having different facial features, although this idea stems from crude and misleading colonial anthropology. The conflict in the Darfur region of Sudan is persistently reported in a racial frame as a conflict between Arabs and Africans.

In India, the Hindu nationalist Bharatyia Janata Party has made a determined effort to heighten the racialization of Indian public culture by proclaiming that the race of 'Aryans' are indigenous to India, thus leaving Muslims as the sole racialized aliens within. The representation of Muslims as racially apart has been buttressed by constructing them as 'Turkish' and 'Persian'. As with racializations elsewhere, there are gendered and sexualized elements to the process. Many Hindus have attributed the supposed decline of their race and civilization to increased emasculation and effeminacy compared to Muslims. The stereotyped notion of Muslims as especially lustful and abnormally adept at multiplying, often borrowing early modern European caricatures, has commonly been used by Hindu nationalists.

Beyond racism and racialized identities: paradoxes and pitfalls

Moving beyond racism will always be hampered by the fact that the combinations of biological determinism, desire for imagined cultural and biological purity, and myths about the immutable qualities of different cultures and ethnicities that are its central features can be packaged and re-packaged in doctrines and practices in a huge, even bewildering variety of ways, although such racisms will also always be destabilized by ambivalence and contradiction.

However, in addition to the reasons already mentioned for the continuing salience of race and racism in the 21st century, two paradoxes of theory and practice deserve mention.

Firstly, the revival of various nationalisms and projects of cultural exclusivity is taking place just at a time when there is an explosion of a multiplicity of cross-cutting transnational, diasporic, ethnic, religious, political, lifestyle, and gender identities. Indeed, there is an intrinsic interconnection between them. We live in a world where individuals can create and re-invent identities and mixtures of identities – the androgynous Michael Jackson's attempted transformation from 'black' to 'white' being only an extreme example. As part of a chronic crisis of 'belonging' in a period of more intensified globalization, a great many individuals are developing loyalties and commitments to a multiplicity of places, cultures, and sexualities beyond traditional ties of nation, ethnicity, and religion. In India, Kolkota soccer fans support Brazil in the World Cup. In Japan, 'black' youth subcultures have developed, with young people wearing their hair in locks, rapping, and using versions of black American street language and fashion.

One reaction against these accelerating dislocations is a desperate attempt by political and cultural elites at closure and mobilization around traditional boundaries. To take one telling example, in November 2003 Denis McShane, Britain's Minister for Europe, urged British Muslims to choose between 'the British way' or the way of (Muslim) terrorists. This is two decades on from the British Conservative politician Norman Tebbit's challenge to British Asians to prove their Britishness by supporting England's cricket team against India and Pakistan.

A long struggle between attempts to create post-ethnic, post-national, post-racial, cosmopolitan frameworks and identities and more backward-looking projects is going to be a continuing feature of life in the 21st century. For the latter, there will continue to be strong temptations and ample opportunities to racialize identities in an effort to shore up traditional cultural loyalties. It will always be possible for them to project powerful images of community that combine physiological markers with cultural practices in a world where the idea of race has long become part of 'common sense' no matter what its scientific credibility. At the level of popular culture, for example, 'monkey chants' by Spanish fans, common against black players, are one of the crudest forms of old racism to continue into the present. Surveys reveal that a large proportion of the black British population believes that it is simply not allowed to feel part of the nation because of its blackness.

Common-sense racial classifications – and here we encounter the second paradox – receive unintended sustenance from census classifications and anti-discrimination legislation. The paradox, of course, is that census classifications and other government surveys in Britain, the USA, and elsewhere use categories such as white, black, mixed, Asian, and so forth partly so that the possible effects of racial discrimination can be monitored by recording patterns of residence, employment, income, and educational achievement. And laws against racialized discrimination have to define who can be accepted as belonging to a 'race' to qualify for protection and redress against unfair discrimination. But enacting 'race' relations legislation and setting up agencies with titles like The Commission for Racial Equality, as we have done in Britain, has had disastrous consequences. In combination with census classifications, they harden crude racial frames of reference by institutionalizing and embedding them in everyday public and private discourse and common sense.

The categories 'mixed' or 'mixed race' are particularly pernicious as they implicitly legitimize the existence of 'pure races'. But confusion is then piled on by allowing geographically derived categories such as 'Asian'.

These categories circulate in governmental discourse, media discussions, and everyday social interaction, allowing the language of race to permeate common sense. The paradox of anti-racism having the effect of assisting the embedding and reproduction of racial classifications is one that bedevils attempts to de-racialize popular culture.

Many Latin American countries claim to have moved beyond race. But Brazil's conception of itself as a 'racial democracy' is itself, paradoxically, a racialized one. And research in Brazil and other Latin American countries has revealed substantial degrees of colour consciousness. Blackness continues to be widely stigmatized, and Brazil has seen the emergence of a variety of forms of black activism to fight discrimination and disadvantage.

The strength of colour consciousness in the USA is one of the most revealing symptoms of the significance of 'race' in the new millennium. The fact that in practice the USA – and almost every European country – still operates some or other version of the 'one drop' rule in relation to blackness but not whiteness, is an anomaly that also acts as a powerful *de facto* recognition of the spurious category of race and the special character of whiteness. Supposed black ancestry 'taints' the individual as black or mixed, while the white ancestry that goes with it is customarily regarded as not allowing the individual to be classified or self-identify as white. This leads to the racialized anomaly in which a white woman can give birth to a black child, but a black mother's child will always be classified as black or mixed.

I end the book with one final consideration, regarding a pitfall that endangers attempts to combat racism. I have not had the space to discuss the efficacy of different anti-racist strategies. But it is necessary to point to the dangerous fallacy involved in one popular conception of racism and racist individuals and its disastrous consequences for challenging racism. This is the common conception of racism as akin to a medical pathology such as a virus infection or a form of cancer. In 2004, Stephen Byers, former Labour Government Cabinet Minister and Chair of the House of Commons Committee against anti-Semitism said, echoing many other judgements, that 'Anti-Semitism is not rational. It is a . . . virus and it mutates. It will not be defeated unless it is treated as a senseless act of hatred that has no logic, no reason and no justification.' But this is to treat racists as suffering from an illness.

It biologizes racists and categorizes them as aliens in the body politic in the same way that extreme racists treat hated ethnic groups as vermin to be exterminated.

If 'race' has less of a hold on the public imagination and has declined in legitimacy over the past hundred years, this is not because an illness of some kind has been eradicated, but because racialized frames of interpretation have been continually challenged and a variety of measures have been put in place to dismantle racially discriminatory practices. Racism is not an irrational aberration. It has emerged in historically specific circumstances and has been inserted into the frames of interpretation and senses of belonging that are intrinsic features of human cultures. Moving beyond racial frames of interpretation is not a medical but a cultural and political project. Ideally, we need to enter a post-national and post-ethnic era. That, however, is another story.

References

In keeping with the style of the Very Short Introduction series, I have kept direct quotations and references to a minimum. To explore in more depth the topics discussed in the book, see Further reading.

Introduction
P-A. Taguieff, *The Force of Prejudice* (University of Minnesota Press, 2001)

Chapter 3
T. Todorov, *The Conquest of America* (Harper and Row, 1984)

Chapter 4
D. Cannadine, *Ornamentalism* (Allen Lane, 2001)
W. Dalrymple, *White Moghuls* (Harper Collins, 2002)
D. Goldhagen, *Hitler's Willing Executioners* (Little, Brown, 1996)
E. Katz, *Confronting Evil* (State University of New York Press, 2004)
A. Nandy, *Intimate Enemy: Loss and Recovery of Self Under Colonialism* (Oxford University Press, 1983)
E. Said, *Orientalism* (Routledge, 1978)

Chapter 5
Hernstein and Murray, *The Bell Curve* (Free Press, 1994)

Chapter 6

F. Halliday, 'Islamophobia Reconsidered', *Ethnic and Racial Studies* 22(5): 892–902

Chapter 7

M. Billig, *Arguing and Thinking: A Rhetorical Approach to Social Psychology* (Cambridge University Press, 1987)

M. Billig, S. Condor, D. Edwards, M.Gane, D. Middleton, and D. Radley, *Ideological Dilemmas* (Sage, 1988)

E. Cashden, 'Ethnocentrism and Xenophobia: A Cross-Cultural Study', *Current Anthropology*, 42 (2001)

S. Pinker, *The Blank Slate: The Modern Denial of Human Nature* (Viking, 2002)

P. Snidermann and E. Carmines, *Reaching Beyond Race* (Harvard University Press, 1997)

J. Tooby and L. Cosmides, *The Adapted Mind: Evolutionary Psychology and the Generation of Culture* (Oxford University Press, 1992)

P. Wachtel, *Race in the Mind of America* (Routledge, 1999)

Chapter 8

C. Brown and P. Gay, *Racial Discrimination: 17 Years After the Act* (Policy Studies Institute, 1985)

M. Brown, M. Carnoy, E. Currie, T. Duster, D. Oppenheimer, M. Shultz, and D. Wellman, *Whitewashing Race: The Myth of a Colour-Blind Society* (University of California Press, 2003)

S. Carmichael and C. Hamilton, *Black Power* (Vintage, 1967)

A. Hacker, *Two Nations: Black and White, Separate, Hostile, Unequal* (Ballantine Books, 1992)

A. Heath and D. McMahon, *Ethnic Differences in the Labour Market* (Oxford Sociology Working Papers, 2000)

I. Macdonald, R. Bhavnani, L. Khan, and G. John, *Murder in the Playground* (Longsight Press, 1989)

D.Massey and N. Denton, *American Apartheid: Segregation and the Making of the Underclass* (Harvard University Press, 1993)

W. MacPherson, *The Stephen Lawrence Inquiry* (London, 1999)

Ali Rattansi, 'Changing the Subject? Racism, Culture and Education', in

J. Donald and A. Rattansi (eds), *'Race', Culture and Difference* (Sage, 1992)

Ali Rattansi, 'Western Racisms, Ethnicities and Identities in a "Postmodern" Frame', in A. Rattansi and S. Westwood (eds), *Racism, Modernity and Identity* (Polity Press, 1994)

Ali Rattansi, 'The Uses of Racialization', in K. Murji and J. Solomos (eds), *Racialization: Studies in Theory and Practice* (Oxford University Press, 2005)

T. Sewell, *Black Masculinities: How Black Boys Survive Modern Schooling* (Trentham Books, 1997)

A. Thernstorm and S. Thernstorm, *America in Black and White: One Nation Indivisible* (Simon and Schuster, 1997)

C. Tilly, *Durable Inequality* (University of California Press, 1998)

W. J. Wilson, *The Declining Significance of Race* (University of Chicago Press, 1978)

W. J. Wilson, *The Bridge Over the Racial Divide* (University of California Press, 1999)

Conclusions

M. Billig, *Banal Nationalism* (Sage, 1995)

N. Ferguson, *The War of the World* (Allen Lane, 2006)

S. Huntington, *The Clash of Civilizations and the Remaking of the World Order* (Simon and Schuster, 1996)

Ali Rattansi, 'New Labour, New Assimilationism', http://www.opendemocracy.net/debates/ article-1-111-2141.jsp

V. Sarich and F. Miele, *Race: The Reality of Human Differences* (Westview Press, 2004)

Further reading

Chapter 2

F. Dikotter (ed.), *The Construction of Racial Identities in China and Japan* (Hurst, 1997)

A. Lindemann, *Anti-Semitism before the Holocaust* (Longman, 2000)

F. Snowden, *Before Colour Prejudice* (Harvard University Press, 1983)

P. Robb (ed.) *The Concept of Race in South Asia* (Oxford University Press, 1995)

Chapter 3

M. Banton, *Racial Theories*, 2nd edn (Cambridge University Press, 1998)

D. Bindman, *Ape to Apollo: Aesthetics and the Idea of Race in the Eighteenth Century* (Reaktion, 2002)

F. Davis, *Who is Black?* (Pennsylvania State University Press, 1991)

S. Fryer, *Staying Power: The History of Black People in Britain* (Pluto Press, 1984)

S. Gilman, 'Black Bodies, White Bodies: Towards an Iconography of Female Sexuality in Late Nineteenth Century Art, Medicine and Literature', in J. Donald and A. Rattansi (eds), *'Race', Culture and Difference* (Sage, 1992)

S. Hall, 'The West and the Rest', in S. Hall and B. Gieben (eds) *Formations of Modernity* (Polity Press, 1992)

I. Hannaford, *Race: The History of an Idea in the West* (Johns Hopkins University Press, 1996)

I. Ignatiev, *How the Irish Became White* (Routledge, 1995)

M. Jacobsen, *Whiteness of a Different Colour: European Immigrants and the Alchemy of Race* (Harvard University Press, 1998)

N. Stepan, 'Race and Gender: The Role of Analogy in Science', in D. Goldberg (ed.) *Anatomy of Racism* (University of Minnesota Press, 1990)

J. Walvin, *Black Ivory: Slavery in the British Empire*, 2nd edn (Blackwell, 2001)

Chapter 4

B. Ashcroft, G. Griffiths, and H. Tiffin (eds), *The Post-Colonial Studies Reader* (Routledge, 1995)

E. Barkan, *The Retreat of Scientific Racism* (Cambridge University Press, 1992)

E. Black, *IBM and the Holocaust* (Random House, 2001)

Z. Bauman, *Modernity and the Holocaust* (Polity Press, 1989)

B. Cohn, *Colonialism and Its Forms of Knowledge* (Princeton University Press, 1996)

D. Cohn-Sherbok, *Understanding the Holocaust* (Continuum, 1999)

N. Dirks, *Castes of Mind: Colonialism and the Making of Modern India* (Princeton University Press, 2001)

A. Gill, *Ruling Passions: Sex, Race and Empire* (BBC Books, 1995)

S. Gilman, *The Jew's Body* (Routledge, 1991)

J. MacKenzie, *Orientalism: History, Theory and the Arts* (Manchester University Press, 1995)

A. McClintock, *Imperial Leather: Race, Gender and Sexuality in the Colonial Contest* (Routledge, 1995)

M. Mann, *Fascists* (Cambridge University Press, 2004)

A. Rattansi, 'Postcolonialism and its Discontents', *Economy and Society*, vol. 26 (1997)

D. Stone, *Constructing the Holocaust* (Valentine Mitchell, 2003)

R. J. Young, *Postcolonialism: An Historical Introduction* (Blackwell, 2001)

Chapter 5

A. Alland Jr, *Race in Mind: Race, IQ and Other Racisms* (Palgrave Macmillan, 2002)

S. Gould, *The Mismeasure of Man*, 2nd edn (Norton, 1996)

M. Kohn, *The Race Gallery: The Return of Racial Science* (Random House, 1995)

Chapter 6

E. Balibar, 'Is There a Neo-Racism?', in E. Balibar and I. Wallerstein (eds), *Race, Nation and Class* (Verso, 1991)

M. Barker, *The New Racism* (Junction Books, 1982)

R. Miles and M. Brown, *Racism*, 2nd edn (Routledge, 2003)

K. Murji and J. Solomos (eds), *Racialization: Studies in Theory and Practice* (Oxford University Press, 2005)

M. Omi and H. Winant, *Racial Formation in the United States* (Routledge, 1986)

Chapter 7

L. Back, *New Ethnicities and Urban Culture* (UCL Press, 1996)

P. Cohen, 'Psychoanalysis and Racism', in D. Goldberg and J. Solomos (eds), *A Companion to Racial and Ethnic Studies* (Blackwell, 2002)

S. Hall, 'The Question of Cultural Identity', in S. Hall, D. Held, and A. McGrew (eds), *Modernity and Its Futures* (Polity Press, 1992)

S. Hall, 'The Spectacle of the Other', in S. Hall (ed.) *Representation* (Sage, 1997)

M. Pickering, *Stereotyping* (Palgrave Macmillan, 2001)

Chapter 8

L. Archer, Race, *Masculinity and Schooling: Muslim Boys and Education* (Open University Press, 2003)

J. Gabriel, *Whitewash: Racialized Politics and the Media* (Routledge, 1998)

O. Gandy Jr, *Communication and Race* (Arnold and Oxford University Press, 1998)

D. Mason (ed.), *Explaining Ethnic Differences* (Policy Press, 2003)

A. Pilkington, *Racial Disadvantage and Ethnic Diversity in Britain* (Palgrave Macmillan, 2003)

A. Rattansi, 'Racism, Sexuality and Political Economy', in S. Fenton and H. Bradley (eds), *Ethnicity and Economy: 'Race and Class' Revisited* (Palgrave Macmillan, 2005)

Conclusions

Z. Baber, 'Race, Religion and Riots: The Racialization of Communal Identity and Conflict in India', *Sociology*, 38, 4 (2004)

R. Bhavnani, H. Mirza, and V. Meetoo, *Tackling the Roots of Racism* (Policy Press, 2005)

P. Fysh and J. Wolfreys, *The Politics of Racism in France*, 2nd edn (Palgrave Macmillan, 2003)

P. Hainsworth (ed.) *The Politics of the Extreme Right* (Pinter, 2000)

D. Hollinger, *Postethnic America*, 2nd edn (Basic Books, 2000)

J. Legge Jr, *Jews, Turks and Other Strangers: The Roots of Prejudice in Modern Germany* (University of Wisconsin Press, 2003)

A. Lentin, *Racism and Anti-Racism in Europe* (Pluto Press, 2004)

B. Parekh, 'Achieving Racial Equality', in G. Loury, T. Madood, and S. Teles (eds), *Ethnicity, Social Mobility and Public Policy* (Cambridge University Press, 2005)

D. Pulera, *Visible Differences: Why Race Will Matter to Americans in the Twenty-First Century* (Continuum, 2003)

H. Winant, *The World is a Ghetto: Race and Democracy Since World War II* (Basic Books, 2001)

Index

Index

Index

Racism